# Hardy Garden Bulbs

# Hardy Garden Bulbs

by

GERTRUDE S. WISTER

*Assistant Director of the Arthur Hoyt
Scott Horticultural Foundation
of Swarthmore College*

E. P. DUTTON & CO., INC.
*New York*

Copyright © 1964 by Gertrude S. Wister   All rights reserved. Printed in the U.S.A.   No part of this book may be reproduced in any form without permission in writing from the publisher, except by a reviewer who wishes to quote brief passages in connection with a review written for inclusion in a magazine, newspaper or broadcast.   Published simultaneously in Canada by Clarke, Irwin & Company Limited, Toronto and Vancouver

# Contents

| | | |
|---|---|---|
| Chapter I | A FIRST LESSON ON BULBS | 11 |
| Chapter II | GENERAL CULTURE | 23 |
| Chapter III | THE SMALL EARLY SPRING BULBS | 35 |
| Chapter IV | HYACINTHS | 53 |
| Chapter V | DAFFODILS | 58 |
| Chapter VI | TULIPS | 96 |
| Chapter VII | BULBS FOR LATE SPRING AND EARLY SUMMER | 121 |
| Chapter VIII | LILIES | 132 |
| Chapter IX | LATE SUMMER AND AUTUMN BULBS | 158 |
| Chapter X | BULBS TO BLOOM INDOORS | 166 |
| Glossary | | 177 |
| Sources of Bulbs | | 183 |
| Good Winter Reading | | 185 |
| Index | | 187 |

# List of Illustrations

## *Drawings*

### (All by Eleanor A. Medford)

| | |
|---|---:|
| A daffodil bulb and its children | 13 |
| A tulip bulb in growth | 13 |
| A lily bulb | 14 |
| A crocus corm, side and bottom | 14 |
| Crocuses in bloom | 43 |
| Winter-aconite | 47 |
| Daffodil forms | 88 |
| Turkscap lily | 133 |
| Upward-facing lilies | 134 |
| Bowl-shaped lilies | 134 |
| Trumpet lilies | 135 |

## *Photographs*

### (All but last by Roche. Last by author.)

#### Following p. 48:

Bulbs ready for planting
Garden flowers which bloom in mid-April
Glory-of-the-snow
*Scilla sibirica* 'Spring Beauty'
Spring star-flower
The summer snowflake
Crocus 'Excelsior'

## List of Illustrations

*Following p. 96:*

A fine collection of daffodils
Wild hybrid of narcissus
Garden hybrid of daffodil
Dutch hyacinths with pansies and English daisies
May-flowering tulips with arabis, hardy candytuft, and pansies
Tulips after digging, showing how each bulb divided
Tulip bulbs packed for summer storage
Hybrids of *Tulipa fosteriana*
*Tulipa turkestanica*

*Following p. 144:*

The Spanish bluebell
Camassias
*Allium rosenbachianum album*
Lily 'Mrs. R. O. Backhouse'
The regal lily
*Colchicum autumnale*
*Cyclamen neapolitanum*
Autumn-flowering crocus

# Hardy Garden Bulbs

CHAPTER I

# A First Lesson on Bulbs

Among the first flower names that a child learns are "crocus," "daffodil," "tulip," and "lily." Among the first flowers a child learns to love and to draw is the crocus, early to bloom after the long winter, colorful and simple for little artists. These same flowers are among the first that the new gardener grows, learning to create colorful pictures out of doors with them, wondering why they sometimes do not come up to expectations, rejoicing when they do.

More often than not, they do indeed come up to expectations, for in the happy world of gardening, some of the most dependable and colorful plants are those the gardener calls "bulbs." In nursery marts and hardware shops, in department stores and five-and-tens, we find them in baskets and crates. Or we order them from catalogs filled with bright pictures, or from plain unornamented lists, and they come to us by mail or express, packed in paper bags, perhaps with shavings, sometimes done up with a little damp peat moss.

These things which we can buy and handle so conveniently, and which we bury so hopefully, imagining all the while the beauty of the flowers we expect them to send forth, are not all true bulbs. But they have certain characteristics in common. They are plants which go through a period when they have no foliage and when the root system generally dies away, to be replaced by a new one. At this time there remain portions of the plant, usually underground, which contain stored food and the parts which will produce roots, leaves, flowers, and seeds. This leafless and rootless period can be greatly extended by digging the plants, curing them, and keeping them out of the ground. During this period, when life processes are held to a minimum, the bulbs can be handled easily and transported long distances to new homes.

Among "bulbs" are to be found plants which grow not only from true bulbs, but also from corms and tubers. It is interesting to know how these three differ from each other.

A bulb may be likened to a bud. It is usually underground, but small bulbs called bulbils sometimes appear in leaf axils, as with tiger lilies, or replace the flower cluster, as with the weed called wild onion or wild garlic. New plants can be grown from bulbils.

An onion sliced in half from top to bottom shows well the bud-like structure. In the center is hidden a group of short pale green leaves, which will emerge from the top as a growing sprout if the onion is kept too long. Surrounding this group of leaves are concentric layers of fleshy tissue which in structure are also leaves, though they will not become green. These white fleshy layers, called *scales,* contain stored food for the growing plant. At the base is a very short cushion-like stem to which they and the small central leaves are joined. Safely enclosed by the scales and by the tiny green leaves is the very heart of the bulb, the future flower.

At the bottom of the stem is a firm area called the *basal plate,* which may have fragments of dried roots clinging to it. The new roots emerge from this basal plate if the onion is planted, and if any portion is damaged, the root system will be smaller. A good healthy intact basal plate is very important. The outermost layer of the bulb is dry and papery, and helps to keep the bulb from drying out. This external layer, or skin, is called a *tunic.* Examples of such tunicated bulbs are daffodils, tulips, and hyacinths.

A lily bulb is constructed differently. It has scales, but they are not enclosed by a tunic, nor are they wrapped in concentric

## A First Lesson on Bulbs 13

layers around a central point. They are quite short and very fleshy, and each is joined separately to a portion of the cushiony stem. Fritillaries also have scaly bulbs, quite similar to those of lilies, to which they are closely related.

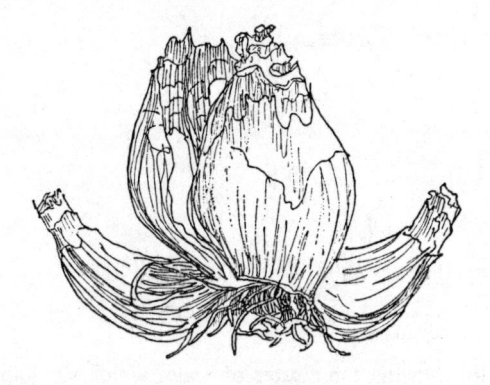

A daffodil bulb and its children. The main bulb is dividing to form two. Two more young bulbs are forming at the sides.

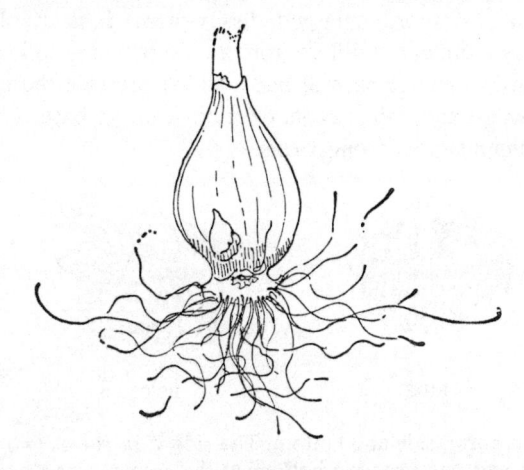

A tulip bulb in growth. (Stem has been cut.) Its roots are active. A new bulb is forming inside the old one, which will disappear. A second new bulb is budding at the base.

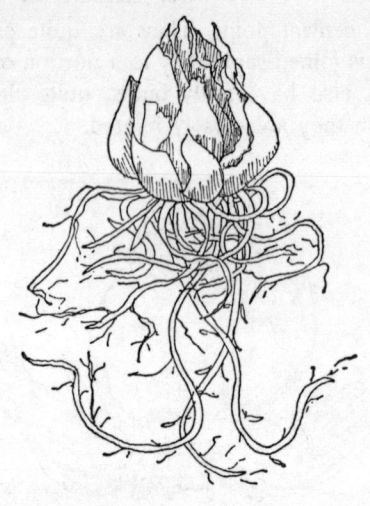

A lily bulb, showing the cluster of scales which are joined at the basal plate, and not protected by an outer wrapping. The fleshy roots have been carefully preserved intact.

A *corm* is a short, enlarged, fleshy stem. It is usually surrounded by a tunic, but differs from a bulb by being solid within. It gives rise to one or several buds, which produce the growing plant aboveground, while roots develop from its base. Crocuses and colchicums grow from corms.

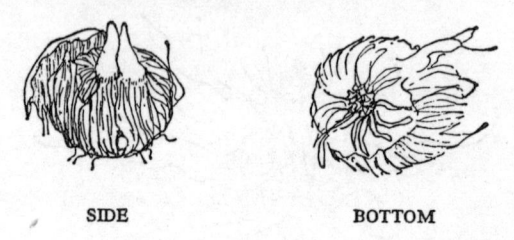

SIDE        BOTTOM

A crocus corm, side and bottom. The side view shows two sprouts at the top and one near the bottom at the center. The dry, papery tunic or outer wrapping is partly loose. Roots are dry and shriveled.

## A First Lesson on Bulbs

A *tuber* is a swollen underground branch or rootstock, containing a supply of stored food. One or more buds can be produced from it, and roots grow from it. Potatoes and Jerusalem artichokes are tubers. The "eyes" are the buds, or growing points, from which stems develop. Cyclamens, winter-aconite, and some of the anemones grow from tubers.

These plant parts are efficient storehouses which serve to maintain the plants during periods that are unfavorable for their active growth aboveground. These may be periods of prolonged cold. Or they may be regular dry seasons, the plants appearing and blooming quite suddenly when rains come. Sometimes bulbous plants come up in haste with the lengthening days of spring. They bloom, set seed, ripen their leaves after storing up a new supply of food, and disappear again before thick tree foliage and the more rampant vegetation of summer have grown enough to shade them out. Many bulbous plants are only visible for three or four months of the year, though they are far from inactive the rest of the time.

The bulbs to be discussed in this book are all hardy; that is, they can withstand a certain amount of freezing weather and ground frozen to a depth of one or two inches for a period of several months. Many are hardy enough to be grown in the northern tier of states and southern Canada; a few only where it is mild enough for plants such as nandinas and camellias to be grown with reasonable success. Such tender plants as gladiolus, dahlias, and tuberous begonias are not discussed. Most of the bulbs included can be grown from coast to coast, except in arid places and those either extremely cold or so warm in winter that the plants have no real dormant season. Further limitations are given for specific bulbs. Most are extremely dependable; others call for a drop of gambling blood and the will to try to satisfy their more exacting requirements.

## BUYING BULBS

A sound bulb is the first step toward a beautiful flower. If you buy sight unseen, patronize a dealer whom you know to be reputable. Do not fall for bargains and extravagant advertising. If you are a novice, buy the dependables for a start.

If you buy locally, patronize the garden center that caters only to garden needs, rather than a hot city store. Bulbs go soft and mushy or dry and hard if exposed for long to a hot, dry atmosphere. Cool, airy storage during the marketing period is important. Examine the bulbs for a firm, healthy appearance, free of mold, bad spots, and blemishes. Buy as early in the season as the bulbs are obtainable.

The bulbs you buy, if they have been properly handled, should contain the rudiments of the flowers which they will produce in their next blooming season. Poor conditions, such as overheating in transit or storage, can destroy these minute buds. After the bulbs are obtained, the bags should be opened at once and put in a cool, airy place until they are planted. Any that are packed in moist material must, of course, be kept moist, but not wet. Prompt planting is essential for these.

Remember that man's efforts have prolonged the bulb's rootless period far beyond the natural time, and that it must be given the opportunity to catch up and make roots before winter. Only tulips can be held out of the ground until late fall to advantage. Lilies are often not shipped until late fall, so that late planting cannot be avoided.

However, late planting is better than no planting at all, as long as the bulbs seem reasonably sound. The flowers of the first season may be dwarfed, or there may not be any bloom. But eventually the plants will recover from their poor start. Frozen ground can often be lifted in layers with a pick, and the bulbs planted in the soft ground underneath. The ground can be mulched to keep it from freezing until planting can be done. Or bulbs can be potted and plunged in compost or in a frame, kept from drying out, and maintained at a temperature too cool for top growth until spring. Then they can be carefully knocked out of the pots and slipped with roots intact into permanent positions.

If any bulbs arrive in poor condition, notify the dealer. If there is a little bluish mold present, shake a little seed disinfectant such as Arasan or Spergon into the bag. Close the bag and turn it about so that the bulbs become coated. Wear gloves when handling dusted bulbs.

Avoid rough handling and dropping of bulbs. Scales can be broken off lily bulbs. Bruises may start decaying spots. If slightly soft bulbs are planted, they may be able to grow out of their trouble, but some may decay completely in the ground. Yet the power of recovery sometimes seems miraculous. I have planted *Scilla sibirica* bulbs so miserable and moldy (one of those bargains) that growth seemed very questionable. But they grew. Two years ago my husband and I debated the planting of two hundred cyclamens, so delayed in transit that they were practically mushy. He won, and they were planted. The following fall there were some leaves and flowers, and this past fall the foliage was much more abundant. Certainly an ample half survived. But if daffodils and lilies had arrived in an equally deplorable state, we would have discarded them.

## A FIRST BULB ORDER

If I were that enviable person, a budding gardener, I would try to turn my first bulb order into a living education. If I could spend an extravagant fifty dollars, I would be able to get a good sampling of the most dependable of the hardy bulbs. For half that, I would have to start picking more carefully. If I had only ten dollars to spend, I would choose the flowers I knew the least, and each year I would try to add something that I was curious about.

For this trial flight, I would buy only half a dozen each of most kinds; of lilies, only one to three. In the spring I would buy a pot of chives to add to my bulb collection, pretending it belonged in the food budget.

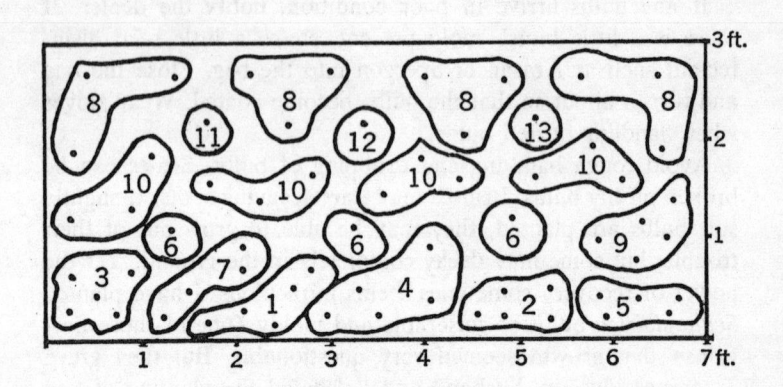

A FIRST BULB BED FOR ABOUT $10

1. 5 *Galanthus nivalis* (Common Snowdrop). Earliest spring
2. 5 *Crocus tomasinianus* (a species crocus). Earliest spring
3. 5 *Chionodoxa luciliae* (Glory-of-the-Snow). Early spring
4. 5 *Tulipa kaufmanniana* (Waterlily Tulip). Early spring
5. 5 *Scilla sibirica* (Siberian Squill). Early spring
6. 3 Dutch Hyacinths, 1 each of 3 varieties. Early spring
7. 5 *Muscari armeniacum* or *botryoides* (Grape-Hyacinth). Mid-spring
8. 12 Daffodils, 3 each of 4 varieties. Early to mid-spring
9. 5 *Scilla campanulata* 'Excelsior.' Mid-spring
10. 12 Tulips, 3 each of 4 varieties. Early to late spring
11. 1 Lily 'Enchantment.' Early summer
12. 1 Lily Olympic Hybrid. Midsummer
13. 1 *Lycoris squamigera* (Hardy Amaryllis). Late midsummer

If you don't like the number 13, call this last the one that makes a baker's dozen. Dealers who handle bulbs in tens charge for five at the ten rate. Those who handle them in dozens charge for six at the dozen rate. If your dealer handles bulbs in dozens, sixes can be planted in the spaces shown for fives.

If I were moving into a newly built house with raw soil, I would have to squeeze out another five dollars for a bale of peat moss. I would pick out a place that seemed to drain well and had at least half a day of sun, and dig up a bed, working in the peat moss thoroughly. Then I would plant the bulbs. The small ones would go in little groups along the front, the others in back. Each group would have a little space around it separating it from the next group, and each kind would have a good legible label. That first spring I would have a chance to study the flowers. Spring bulbs could be taken up in summer to make way for a more permanent development of the place, or they could be left for a few years. Pansies could be planted between the bulbs for spring bloom and to give a chance to study color combinations; annuals could be added when danger of frost was over. If annuals are to go directly over bulbs, they should either be sown as seed or planted small enough to prevent injury to the bulbs.

Here is a list of dependables. All are described in the course of the book. They are arranged in approximate blooming order.

In the lists throughout the book, *italic type* denotes botanical names; single quotation marks (*Galanthus nivalis* 'S. Arnott') designate a horticultural variety or cultivar (*see* Glossary). Double quotation marks are used for names that are in common use, but which are not the preferred or officially accepted names.

In extensive lists of cultivars, the single quotation marks have been omitted.

| | |
|---|---|
| EARLIEST SPRING | Snowdrops (*Galanthus nivalis*) |
| | *Crocus tomasinianus* (a species) |
| EARLY SPRING | Dutch Crocuses (choose two colors, six of each) |
| | *Tulipa kaufmanniana* (a species) |
| | Glory-of-the-Snow (*Chionodoxa luciliae*) |
| | Siberian Squill (*Scilla sibirica*) |

| | |
|---|---|
| MID-SPRING | Grape-Hyacinth (*Muscari armeniacum* or 'Heavenly Blue') |
| | Dutch Garden Hyacinths (perhaps six mixed) |
| | Summer Snowflake (*Leucojum aestivum*) |
| EARLY TO LATE SPRING | Daffodils in order of bloom, five from the following list: February Gold, Fortune, Insurpassable, Aranjuez, John Evelyn, Mrs. R. O. Backhouse, Cheerfulness, Thalia, Trevithian, Actaea |
| EARLY TO LATE SPRING | Tulips. As soon as possible, try a variety from each division listed in the chapter on tulips. To begin with, choose one or two from Division 2, 3, or 5; one or two from 6, 8, 9, or 10; and one or two from 7, 14, 15, 18, 19, 20, or 23 |
| MID-SPRING | *Scilla campanulata* 'Excelsior' |
| LATE SPRING | Dutch Iris (one or two kinds) but only south of Washington, D.C., or where your local dealer tells you they will succeed outdoors |
| EARLY SUMMER | Mid-Century Hybrid Lilies |
| MIDSUMMER | Olympic Hybrid Lilies |
| LATE SUMMER | Aurelian hybrid lilies (*see* page 146) |
| | Hardy Amaryllis (*Lycoris squamigera*) |
| AUTUMN | *Colchicum autumnale* |
| | *Crocus speciosus* |

## KEEP A NOTEBOOK

A loose-leaf notebook becomes a useful repository of your garden experience. Keep a record of orders, blooming dates, observations on your own garden and plants seen other places.

Write down while it is fresh in your mind what you would like to try in new kinds, in color combinations. Record the changes you want to make. Draw little sketches or plans of what you have already and of what you would like to have. It is easy in spring to think you can remember just how the garden looks, but by the time irises and roses have come and gone, you will not remember as well as you thought you would.

Labels are a valuable guide, but they do meet with accidents, especially from children and sometimes from dogs. Kinds that can be hidden inconspicuously and kept close to the ground are the safest.

## THE SPECIAL PLANT SOCIETIES

There are many societies which have been formed by people interested in certain groups of flowers, and several of these are devoted entirely or partly to hardy bulbous plants. Membership in them is usually about five dollars a year. They issue publications, hold national and regional meetings, sponsor flower shows and garden visits. In addition, membership gives a chance for those who are interested in the same flower and who live near each other to become acquainted.

The society memberships are made up of both men and women, amateurs, professionals, and commercial growers. All profit from the pleasure of knowing each other. The most ignorant beginner is welcome. Since the officers change often, a good way to find out how to join a society is to write to the editor of a garden magazine or of a newspaper garden column for the name and address of the society's secretary.

American Daffodil Society
American Iris Society (partly)    Mostly non-bulbous iris
American Rock Garden Society (partly)    Mostly non-bulbous plants
National Tulip Society
North American Lily Society
American Plant Life Society (partly)    Mostly tender plants

## "ASK THE PLANT"

There is an old horticultural story about the person who wrote to a horticultural expert asking how much fertilizer to put on a certain plant. The answer was, "Ask the plant." In other words, rules and advice must be adapted to your plant growing under the conditions of its particular spot. Not only is your garden different from mine, even though I may live next door, but the place by your front door is different from the place by your back door. Of course there are great similarities, too, in gardens in Maine, Virginia, and Iowa. Even California, Texas, Georgia, and Oregon can be added to that list. People in all those states and many more belong to the American Daffodil Society. The lady from Tulsa says to the man from Pennsylvania, "We can't do it the way you do." But both do grow daffodils, and many others of the same bulbs.

There is a tremendous amount to be learned from books, and no gardener can do without them, but your plants, too, will teach you. I have always thought that to be a good gardener, first of all you must have a green heart, and next you must have a green mind. These combined with a little muscle are needed to produce a green thumb and a beautiful garden.

# CHAPTER II

# General Culture

### SOILS

The most dependable bulbs grow in any average well-drained soil. With attention to planting where drainage is good, most people can enjoy beautiful flowers from bulbs without any trouble.

But many, as their interest grows, want to grow better flowers, and more kinds, including some that are more difficult to please. Soil improvement is the first step in the right direction. A good soil gives real gardening joy. It produces fine flowering trees and shrubs, good vegetables, and well-filled, flourishing flower beds. It nurtures extensive, efficient root systems that are able to withstand other unfavorable conditions.

Two aspects of the soil must be considered: its physical condition and its chemical content. A soil in good physical condition is easy to dig. It does not become caked or hard in dry weather, or soggy and waterlogged in wet weather. It lets excess water drain away quickly, yet it retains plenty of moisture to tide plants over dry spells. The particles that compose it are not so tightly packed that roots cannot easily find their way among them.

The physical condition of the soil is determined by the sizes of the mineral particles and the amount and kind of organic matter in it. It is also affected by the drainage. The chemical condition is determined by the chemical composition of the soil particles and of the organic matter. Some of the chemicals necessary for plant nutrition may be used slowly by the plants through the years as they become dissolved in the soil water. Some may be in very insoluble and therefore unusable form. They are, we then say, not available. While certain bacteria and other unseen organisms in the soil, as well as acids secreted by the roots, work to make nutrients available slowly, they cannot break down these insoluble compounds.

If soil is in poor physical condition, chemical fertilizers will not help it. It must be improved by the addition of organic matter and by correcting any faulty drainage. This is an all-over operation involving deep cultivation and thorough incorporation of plenty of organic material. It is not enough to put a handful of sand under each bulb and dig a little peat moss around it. The entire area needs attention. Peat moss in quantity, also leaf mold, compost, and processed (not ordinary) manures, are all suitable for improving the soil for bulbs.

## PRINCIPAL KINDS OF SOIL

*Sandy soils* are made up of coarse mineral particles. They are apt to be low in plant nutrients and in organic matter, and they drain so well that they rapidly lose the nutrients added in fertilizers. They are easy to work. They dry out fast. They warm up quickly in spring. A spoonful of sandy soil shaken up in water settles out in a short time.

*Clay soils* are the other extreme, composed of particles so fine that a damp pinch rubbed in the fingers feels velvety. A spoonful shaken up in water stays in suspension for a long time, making the water cloudy. They are apt to cake in dry weather, to pack hard if walked on when wet. They are heavy to dig, and digging them when they are wet results in the formation of hard clods that are difficult to break up. They drain poorly, and are late to warm up in spring. But usually they are quite high in the elements needed for plant nutrition, if these can become available.

Both sands and clays can be greatly improved by the addition of organic matter, and added sand helps to break up clay. Lime also is used to improve clay soils. The amount to be used must be determined by a soil test and by considering the other plants grown in the flower bed. If azaleas and other plants that need an acid soil are there, lime must be used with caution and placed where it will not affect them. You can have a soil test made by taking or sending a sample of about a pint of soil to your county agricultural agent. He can be reached through your local courthouse. Take a good mixture of soil from several parts of your property and from depths of a foot as well as near the surface.

*Silts* come between the extremes of sands and clays. They are less of a problem, but still often deficient in organic matter, and need the same type of treatment as clay to bring them into good garden condition.

## ORGANIC MATTER

Organic matter occurring naturally in the soil comes from animal and vegetable remains. Properly, this organic matter should be in a continual state of disintegration and be continually renewed as roots die and are replaced, as leaves fall and disintegrate, as whole plants die, and as animal remains are deposited as excrement, bones, or shells. A good supply of organic material in the soil aids in its porosity, which enables it to admit water and air freely. The excess water is able to drain through, but much is absorbed so that plants can use it as it is needed. In clays, organic matter assists drainage; in sands, it retards drying out.

The soil air is important, too. It contains carbon dioxide which, with the soil water, helps through the formation of carbonic acid to dissolve chemicals slowly for plant use.

## THE SUBSOIL

We may have a layer of good soil, and still have poor growing conditions because of a bad subsoil. In contrast to the top layer, which is full of activity from growing roots, teeming bacteria, worms, and so forth, the subsoil is relatively inert. It may be a compacted layer called hardpan, difficult for even tree roots to penetrate, extremely dry in droughts and soggy in wet spells. Trees uprooted in storms often disclose this condition. When deep trenches are dug across a property, they are worth examination, for they can disclose the secrets of the subsoil.

Sometimes the subsoil must be broken up, but for many bulbs, good topsoil and well-drained subsoil need not be as deep as for larger plants. Small bulbs, such as crocuses and snowdrops, need only six inches or so, but for larger bulbs soil should be moderately good to the depth of a foot, and eighteen inches is better.

## IMPORTANCE OF GOOD DRAINAGE

Good drainage is so important for the successful growing of bulbs that it deserves a little extra emphasis. Many bulbs originate in places where they are well baked during hot, dry summers. Grown in places of more summer moisture, and especially in gardens that may receive artificial watering, they may suffer from an excess of water during the time they are without foliage.

To facilitate drainage, heavy subsoil should be broken up with a pick and some kind of organic matter worked into it. Sometimes tile drains may be needed to lead excess water to points where it will not interfere with plant growth by creating a stagnant, airless condition. Avoid planting bulbs in low spots, or where water finds its way as it moves from higher ground. Slopes are not always well drained, especially in the spring.

Often the bulb-growing situation may be improved by raising the level of the area to be planted: just a few inches may make a big difference. A stone edge to support the higher level may add a great deal to the attractiveness of the garden. In a formal setting, it should be of dressed stones laid neatly to conform with the garden atmosphere. But it is often possible to use stones quite irregular in shape, laid informally. Low retaining walls built of several thin layers of stone laid without mortar can be used either formally or informally with pleasing results.

## WATER

In spite of all that has been said about the need for drainage, there are special times when bulbs need an assured and adequate supply of moisture. First of all, they need it during the period when they should be making new roots. While it is reasonably safe to plant bulbs in a dry soil and wait for rain, a good watering will start rooting sooner. Anything that comes packed in moist material should most certainly not be allowed to dry out before or after planting. Bulbs that have the reputation of being difficult should have special attention to be sure that they have sufficient moisture while they are becoming established, which means a good watering every once in a while during their first autumn until winter sets in.

Then too, when growth starts in the spring, a hot dry spell can be cruel. Fast-developing plants should not be allowed to suffer for lack of moisture. Young stems can be soft, so use a canvas or perforated hose or some other method of soil soaking instead of an overhead sprinkler. Water must be sufficient to penetrate to the root level. During dry spells after flowering, a soaking now and then will extend the life of the foliage, and enable it to make better bulbs for the next year. Many bulbs have lived in many gardens for a long time without this extra care, but it does make a difference in quality.

## FERTILIZERS

A soil that is well drained and adequately provided with organic matter is easy to work and likely to provide good flowers year after year without the addition of extra fertilizer. However, if top growth and exhibition bloom are wanted, fertilizers may be used. Where soils are low in phosphorus (ask your county agent about this in your area), it is wise to add superphosphate, digging it well into the spots to be planted, at the rate of four pounds per hundred square feet. Bone meal may be used as a source of phosphorus, but it is more expensive.

A complete nitrogen-phosphorus-potash fertilizer may be used, but a formula low in nitrogen is preferable, such as a 4-12-8. (This means 4% nitrogen, 12% phosphorus, and 8% potash available for plant use.) Sometimes a fertilizer containing no nitrogen at all is used, such as 0-20-20. The fertilizer can be dug in before planting, or if bulbs are to be interspersed through a bed already planted, forked just into the patches where the bulbs are to go.

I would rather under- than over-fertilize, but it is always hard to tell how much fertilizer to use. A moderate sprinkle of the average fertilizer is enough at one time. The highly concentrated ones must be used very lightly, and the directions on the container should be followed. Mix the fertilizer thoroughly with the soil. In the spring, just as the new growth is emerging, fertilizer can be sprinkled around the plants. Scratch it into the top layer of soil if possible. Do not let it stay on foliage. Hose or shake it off before it has a chance to burn.

While manures are sources of plant food as well as of organic matter, even well-rotted manures are not the best choice for bulbs. Not only are they apt to introduce many weed seeds, but they may foster disease. They are high in one plant growth element, nitrogen, and deficient in two others, phosphorus and potash. Dried and bagged manures are treated to kill the weed seeds, and often have had phosphorus and potash added in some form. The analysis can be found on the bags. Even dried manures should not be in contact with the bulbs. If they are used to improve the soil before planting, they should be very thoroughly mixed several weeks before planting so that some of the nitrogen may be dissipated. Manure plays an important part in the Netherlands in bulb production, but skilled Dutch growers with their cool climate and sandy soil are better able to use it properly than is the average American amateur. As far as soil improvement goes, dried and packaged manures are an expensive way to add humus or organic material.

### SUN

Bulbs vary in their need for sun. In general, they must have sun or ample light for several hours a day in order to store up food to last them until the next growing period. Early spring bulbs can often be planted under trees as long as they receive sun before tree foliage is expanded. As the spring advances, a little light shade in the afternoon will prolong bloom, because it shades the flowers from early hot spells during the warmest part of the day.

Bulbs often grow very well under the high shade of tall trees, but trees and shrubs with thick branches near the ground can give too dense a shade for good bloom. In flower beds, bulb foliage cannot fulfill its function if smothered by neighboring perennials before it has ripened.

EXTENDING TIME OF BLOOM. Sun is especially important in advancing the first bloom. A sunny spot against a wall can be used to advance spring by a week or two. Use the very earliest varieties in such a spot. A little later in the season, the same location might be too hot for bulbs and the flowers might complete their bloom too quickly. A cool location, perhaps a northern slope, will delay flowering time. These differences should be used to prolong garden interest. By making use of the different exposures around our own small house, we have had winter-aconite in bloom from February 18 (in a very cold spring) until April 15.

## PLANTING

If a number of kinds of bulbs are to be planted, sketch out a planting scheme in advance, and put a label to show where each kind is to go before tumbling the bulbs out of their bags.

Fork over the space to be planted, breaking up lumps and working in organic matter and fertilizer if necessary. Then it is a quick job to dig the holes for the individual bulbs with a trowel or a narrow garden spade. First set the bulbs in place on top of the ground, then plant each one to the proper depth. Be sure the holes are wide enough at the bottom for the bulbs to rest on firm earth, instead of having air spaces under them. Even though the aim is to plant them right side up, if they happen to fall over, they will grow anyway. Fill around the bulbs with earth so that no air spaces are left. Firm the earth, or water well to settle it.

If a mass planting of uniform appearance is wanted, the whole area can be dug, removing the earth to an even depth. The bulbs are placed at the proper intervals and the earth carefully thrown back over them, bringing the level back to the proper point.

Many bulbs are planted in an informal way called "naturalizing." They are scattered and grouped in grass, woods, or under shrubs in such a way that it looks as if they grew there of their own accord, without any plan or action by the gardener. Any forced look must be avoided. Naturalizing cannot be carried out successfully in a place where the grass must be cut before the bulb foliage has ripened. Planting distances between naturalized bulbs should not be uniform. Grouping should be irregular, and any straight rows avoided. Daffodils, grape-hyacinths, and both early and late scillas look very well planted this way, and can be left undisturbed indefinitely.

A mattock, a pick with a broad blade which can be used to make a hole about four inches wide, can often be used for planting bulbs in naturalizing. A clod of earth is lifted back and held long enough for the bulb to be dropped into the hole, then allowed to drop back over it.

DEPTH AND SPACING. Distances given below are the depth of soil over the top of the bulb. Measure the length of your trowel so that it can serve as a guide in planting.

An inch one way or the other does not make a noticeable difference in the average bulb planting. However, in sandy or in deep, mellow, well-prepared soils, plant a little deeper. Shallow planting of tulips and daffodils and probably some other bulbs causes the bulbs to divide more rapidly. The result is many small bulbs that do not grow to blooming size before dividing again.

TWO TO THREE INCHES  Small bulbs. Snowdrops, small scillas, grape-hyacinths, chionodoxas, crocuses, spring snowflakes, cyclamens, winter-aconite, anemones, madonna lilies, the tiniest daffodils.

THREE TO FOUR INCHES  Daffodils that always make small bulbs (some of the species and some varieties), the larger scillas, bulbous iris, base-rooting lilies, summer snowflakes, smaller alliums, colchicums.

FOUR TO FIVE INCHES  Tulips, daffodils, stem-rooting lilies, larger alliums, *Lycoris squamigera.*

There are many considerations in deciding distances to be left between bulbs. Those to remain undisturbed for many years should be farther apart than those planned for short-term mass effect. The size of the flowers must be taken into consideration. Long-flowered trumpet lilies must be far enough apart so that the flowers will not touch each other. Tulips planted to give a blaze of solid color should be quite close. There will be further discussion of these matters in later chapters.

## PESTS AND DISEASES

For the most part, bulbous plants are, happily, free of troubles. However, trouble can occur, and it is best to know what to watch for. The ones that can be serious are discussed later in relation to the particular plants affected. Watch out for plants that are stunted or distorted. Any that are found should be dug out promptly, dropped directly into a paper bag as a precaution against scattering disease organisms, and burned.

Rodents are especially fond of tulips, crocuses, and lilies, and may make it practically impossible to have them in the garden. Chipmunks, squirrels, rabbits, and mice all do their share of damage. Live trapping and banishment to a good distance may help with all but mice, but will have to be repeated as newcomers move in. Bulbs may be planted in wire baskets, but rabbits will eat leaves and flowers and tender lily shoots. Poison wheat can be placed in mole runs, which are used by mice, and placed under coverings that will keep it away from birds. I have noticed that birds usually leave the wheat that is in bird seed, but the squirrels eat it. Naphthalene flakes can be sprinkled around bulbs to act as a repellent, but must be renewed. I do not think the flakes last long enough to do much good, and if they are used too copiously they may injure the bulbs. There are a number of rabbit repellents on the market. They seem to help, but must be renewed, especially after rain. I have a friend who pins her faith to soft-drink bottles sunk in the earth near threatened plants with just an inch or two of the bottle above ground level. The soft whistle in the bottles is said to frighten rabbits away. Wire fine enough to keep small rabbits out or twiggy branches laid around blooming plants are probably more effective.

Chipmunks and squirrels are most likely to dig up bulbs soon after planting, when the ground is soft. Hardware cloth (the kind often used over cellar windows) laid over a planted area will discourage digging until the ground freezes.

Traps and special baits can be used against moles. Success with them varies. It is also possible to grub-proof lawns with one of the products designed for the purpose, which sends the moles looking for their dinner in fresh pastures. But the far-reaching effect of these poisons disturbs many people.

Fortunately, there are many lovely plants which are not bothered by rodents. Daffodils, colchicums, snowdrops, scillas, and chionodoxas are among them.

We hear more and more these days about nematodes or eelworms. These are minute worm-like creatures that often infest plants and cause various unhealthy symptoms such as dwarfing, leaf malformations, yellow blotches on hyacinth leaves, and blisters on daffodil leaves. If you have good reason to suspect nematode trouble, consult your county agricultural agent. Nematode control is an important part of modern bulb production, and the stock bought from reliable sources should be free of these pests.

## CARE OF FOLIAGE

The foliage of a bulb has to do its job in a comparatively short time. It must supply food for the growing and blossoming plant and perhaps for the ripening seed, and it must send food to the bulb for the formation of next year's incipient leaves and flowers, for a new root system, and the first growth of the next season. It also contributes to the increase of the bulb. Notice that if a seed pod is left to develop, the foliage stays green longer than if the faded flower is removed.

When the work of the foliage is over, the final supply of food has been transferred to the bulb. The leaves turn yellow, then brown and withered, and can then be removed.

The removal of faded flowers is usually not important, but if those of the larger bulbs are unsightly, snap them off just below the bloom. The stalk is green and functions like a leaf; it may remain, even though it does not bear leaves. If tulip flowers are removed to help control disease (*see* "Diseases" in tulip chapter, page 101, snap the flowers off before the petals fall, or gather up fallen petals.

The flowers of many bulbs are on scapes, which are leafless flower stalks, and picking the flowers does not deprive the bulbs of foliage. But some others have both leaves and flowers on the same stalk. Tulips and lilies, which make such handsome cut flowers, must be picked with short stems if the bulbs are not to suffer. Tulips should be cut with only the top leaf, or two leaves at the most. Only the top third of a lily stalk should be cut. Of course if the bulb is to be replaced with a new one, it does not matter how much foliage is cut.

CHAPTER III

# The Small Early Spring Bulbs

The forerunners of spring do not wait for balmy days, but push up through frozen ground as the days lengthen. Warm spells in late winter will hurry them, so their blooming period is quite variable. Snowdrops, winter-aconite, the earliest crocuses, and the little blue *Iris histrioides major* sometimes bloom at our home near Philadelphia in late January, but in cold years it may be the end of February before they are in bloom, and early March before they are at their height. With the earliest flowers, location has great influence.

After these first hardy blossoms have appeared, there is a succession of small bulbs that are delightful and dependable, and other small bulbs of charm but unpredictable behavior. They are presented in this chapter in two groups, each following as closely as possible the time of bloom, except that crocuses are treated separately at the end of the first section. The first part (snowdrops to crocuses) covers the bulbs that are commonly reliable. The second part (winter-aconite to *Erythronium*) includes those that are more fastidious in their requirements.

## BLOOMING DATES

Although flowers are listed in sequence, the blooming periods overlap. They also vary somewhat from year to year, though they are consistent enough for approximate times of bloom to be given. In a mixed planting of bulbs and other plant material, there may be disappointment in some years when a planned combination does not materialize because one of its components flowers at the wrong time.

In the South, spring comes more slowly, and the flowering times are spread out over several months that are compressed into a few weeks in the North, where spring comes with a rush. I have tried to give an approximation of blooming dates by use of the terms Early Spring, Mid-Spring, and so forth.

Early bulbs can be used to advance spring bloom by a good month over that of the average home planting. It is not convenient to have small bulbs in a flower bed where late spring and summer flowers are grown, but there are many other places where they can grow year after year without disturbance. They can go under trees where grass is skimpy, in rock gardens and semi-wild gardens, in front of shrubs, and in woodlands.

Except when other depths are given, bulbs in this chapter should be covered with two or three inches of soil and planted two to four inches apart. Their main requirement after planting is to be left alone to bloom and increase. Sometimes clumps become overcrowded, or the growth of other plants makes transplanting advisable. Snowdrops, scillas, and other low, vigorously growing plants can be lifted with a trowel or spade and transferred at once to a new location. If the clumps are thick, dividing is advisable, but it is best to wait for this until the flowers have faded. Dig the clump, gently separate it into smaller portions, and replant. Water at planting time, and again if the soil becomes dry.

Clumps can also be taken up for more complete division

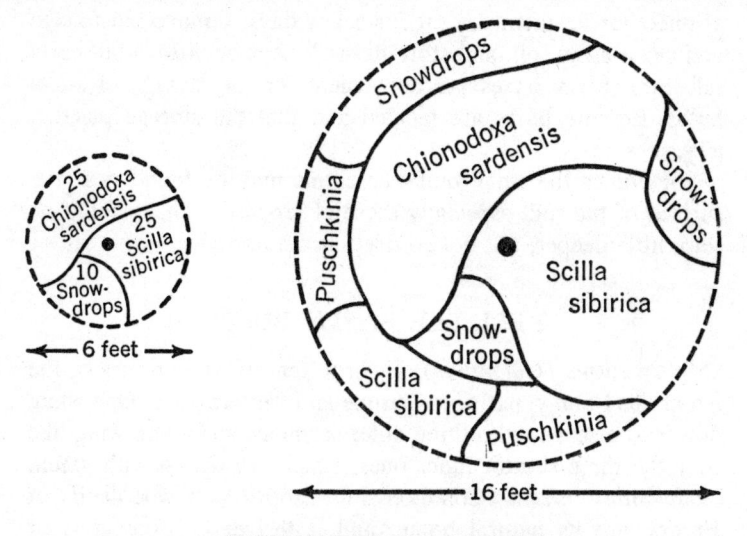

## EARLY SPRING BLOOM
## UNDER A FLOWERING DOGWOOD

On the left is a diagram of the ground under a small dogwood. The bulbs can be planted rather far apart to be distributed through their allotted space. The scillas and chionodoxas will seed, filling the gaps, and spread out as the tree grows. The snowdrops will grow slowly into clumps, but more will need to be added in the new spaces.

Small clumps of the other bulbs can be transplanted to cover the enlarging area, or some new ones planted. One or two additional kinds might be wanted.

On the right is a diagram of the ground under the same tree as it might be ten or twelve years later. The same principle of planting can be applied to other small flowering trees.

These little bulbs can give six or more weeks of spring bloom before the tree comes into leaf.

when the foliage starts to turn yellow. Pull apart and replant at once. Or let them dry off for a few days, remove old foliage and clean away soil, and store in mesh bags or boxes until early fall. Strawberry boxes are convenient for the storage of small bulbs. Be sure bulbs are labeled and that the storage place is airy.

Sometimes the small bulbs or corms may be found near the surface of the soil, especially those of crocuses. They should be set a little deeper, but not so deep as mature ones.

## RELIABLE EARLY BULBS

SNOWDROPS (*Galanthus*). Eight to ten bulbous species of the Amaryllis Family, native to Europe and western Asia. One white flower to a scape, with three outer segments spreading wing-like over the three shorter inner ones, which are tipped with green.

*Galanthus nivalis,* Common Snowdrop. Open woodlands of Europe are its natural home, and it thrives in woodlands or shady corners here. The flowers are about an inch long on scapes 4 or 5 inches long. The leaves are about a quarter of an inch wide. It blooms in late winter or early spring, pushing up through frozen ground, much influenced by exposure and warm spells of late winter. If your neighbor's snowdrops bloom either earlier or later than yours, though apparently not because of different exposures, trade a few bulbs. There are forms that bloom at different times. Two desirable varieties are 'Atkinsii' and 'S. Arnott,' both tall, vigorous, and of fine form.

The double form (*G. nivalis flore-pleno*) is a curiosity. Just a few are enough.

*G. elwesii,* Giant Snowdrop. Asia Minor and the Aegean area. The flowers are larger than those of the common snowdrop, on scapes about 10 inches high. The leaves are nearly an inch wide. It does well in woodlands.

These are the two snowdrops commonly offered in this country. The common snowdrop is the best choice for large plantings. It is the cheapest, and grows into clumps that are easy to divide and replant immediately as soon as the flowers have faded. The giant snowdrop is large enough to give good contrast to it.

Snowdrops can be planted by the dozen or by the hundred, depending on space available. While they do need sun in the spring, summer shade makes no difference to them.

SNOWFLAKES (*Leucojum*). Nine or ten species, bulbous, of the Amaryllis Family. They are closely related to snowdrops, but differ in having six tepals of equal length, instead of a set of three long ones and a set of three short ones. They are natives of Europe and the Mediterranean area.

*Leucojum vernum,* Spring Snowflake. Europe. It blooms right after the snowdrops, and at a little distance might be mistaken for one. The six white segments are tipped with green that turns yellow as the flowers age. Flowers come singly or sometimes two on scapes up to 8 inches high. In a humus-rich, well-drained location, it grows into large clumps, and also seeds itself. Plants bought under this name sometimes turn out to be the summer snowflake, *L. aestivum.*

*L. aestivum,* Summer Snowflake. The flowers of this species are borne in a cluster of two to five that spray out from the top of a scape about a foot high. They are white, green-tipped, and bell-like, about 3/4 of an inch long. The variety 'Gravetye' ('Gravetye Giant') is more robust, with larger flowers.

The summer snowflake is long-lived, increasing slowly into large clumps. It is good for partly shaded garden spots, and while it is not showy enough to inspire mass planting in a season when bloom is becoming plentiful, it is another pretty and graceful flower for mid-spring, not summer, when it blooms with grape-hyacinths and daffodils. Cover the bulbs three to four inches, and plant four to five inches apart.

SQUILLS (*Scilla*). Scillas divide quite easily into the early-blooming squills and later-blooming species. As considered here, they comprise about ninety species of the Old World, and belong to the Lily Family, with narrow leaves.

*Scilla sibirica,* Siberian Squill. Easy to buy, easy to plant, easy to grow, and easy to look at. This is an indispensable. The bright blue buds thrust through thawing ground, finally opening into flaring bells that droop one to three to a scape 3 to 5 inches high.

This is a sturdy bulb to plant under trees where grass does not thrive, for first the flowers will spread a sheet of piercing blue, and then the leaves a covering of green, before the tree leaves develop. Try a few dozen of these under a dogwood, magnolia, or Japanese maple. They seed freely, so soon you will have a mushrooming population. Put a few bulbs in all sorts of odd corners so that you can start to collect dividends as soon as possible. 'Spring Beauty,' a variety a little taller with a tinge of violet in its blue, is handsome and floriferous, and grows into large clumps, but does not seem to set seed.

*S. sibirica alba.* This white form seeds freely, too. On our place the blue and white squills were originally planted in separate patches. Now, ten years later, they are in a delightful jumble, bordering the drive, creeping under shrubs and low trees, and spilling down a low hillside a little farther each year. Some are dug up in the course of gardening operations, but they grow and bloom on top of the ground.

*S. tubergeniana.* This gives the effect of off-white, but is palest blue. It is vigorous and free-flowering, different enough from *S. sibirica* to make it worthwhile to plant a few. It is said to bloom with snowdrops and winter-aconite, but we have never had it that early.

*S. bifolia.* This is less vigorous than *S. sibirica,* and differs from it in its earlier bloom, its rather variable color, usually bright blue, and in having starry flowers with strongly reflexed tepals, several to a scape.

GLORY-OF-THE-SNOW (*Chionodoxa*). Five or six species of small bulbous plants of the Lily Family from Crete and Asia

Minor. They bloom with the early scillas, and are quite like them in size and general effect, but are blessed with a little extra loveliness. The ones usually available are from Turkey, where they bloom at the edge of the receding snow. The flowers are starry and look outward, or up at the sky. They increase and set seed with welcome abandon.

*Chionodoxa gigantea.* The flowers are light blue with a white eye, several to a 4- to 6-inch stem. The flowers (not giants) are about 1¾ inches across. *Alba* is a lovely pure white variety.

*C. luciliae.* It is a little smaller than *C. gigantea,* blue or lavender-blue. There are pink and white forms, the white one more effective.

*C. sardensis.* This is a darker and more intense blue, with a dozen or more small flowers, each with a tiny white eye, on a 7-inch scape.

*C. tmoli (tmolusi).* Resembles *C. luciliae,* but is a little smaller and brighter.

GRAPE-HYACINTHS (*Muscari*). Small bulbous plants of the Lily Family, natives of the Mediterranean area and southwest Asia. The slender, rather fleshy leaves appear in autumn and are hardy, though the ends are sometimes killed back an inch or so. The slender clusters of closely set narrow-mouthed blue bells look like the clusters of grapes that give them their common name. They are called "bluebottles" by the children, who love to pick them in the fields. These open in mid-spring.

*Muscari armeniacum.* Bright deep violet-blue; scapes 4 to 8 inches high. A strong species that is very effective. Its variety 'Heavenly Blue' is a vigorous grower and perhaps a shade darker.

*M. botryoides.* Violet-blue, scapes 4 to 8 inches high. It is naturalized from New England to Minnesota, and south to Virginia and Kansas, an indication of its vigor in our climate. The white form shows off best among other low plants of other colors. It is not effective naturalized.

*M. tubergenianum.* Called the Oxford and Cambridge grape-hyacinth, because of the light Cambridge-blue flowers at the top of the spike and the dark Oxford-blue flowers at the bottom.

*Hyacinthus azureus* ("Muscari azureum," *Hyacinthella azurea*). This is usually listed in catalogs with the *Muscari,* which it greatly resembles. It is delightful, producing fat clusters of tiny blue bells to about 6 inches high, earlier than the true grape-hyacinths. The white form is equally charming.

Grape-hyacinths are of a stature and color that make them excellent foils for daffodils and tulips. Groups of them interspersed in front of these taller flowers, and between varieties, set them off to perfection. They can be naturalized in grass that is not cut too early (the blues rather than the whites), clustered at the edges of shrub plantings, and in lightly shaded semi-wild plantings.

PUSCHKINIA. A genus of two or three species, belonging to the Lily Family, of the Caucasian region and Asia Minor. The only one commonly grown is the Lebanon squill or striped squill (*Puschkinia scilloides,* sometimes listed as *P. libanotica*). When this is thriving, it bears as many as fifteen starry flowers, pale blue or white softly striped blue, on scapes about 7 inches high. It flourishes for years in shady situations that do not dry out, but does not do well in hot, dry places. At its best it looks more like a small hyacinth than the scilla whose name it has borrowed. It blooms with the scillas and chionodoxas.

## CROCUS

This important genus contains some seventy-five species of corm-producing plants, natives of the Mediterranean region and southwest Asia. It belongs to the Iris Family. The leaves are slender and grassy, each with a pale midrib. The stem is very short, not coming aboveground. What appears to be the stem is the perianth tube of the flower. It is worth sacrificing a flower to curiosity. Tear the tepals gently apart, and the style can be seen, extending down to the ovary where the seeds are produced, at ground level or below it.

The crocus corm is wrapped in a brownish tunic, and the corm itself is composed of solid white starchy material, unfortunately considered very good eating by rodents. One or more buds develop from the corm, and as each one grows, a new corm develops at the surface of the old corm, which gradually shrivels up.

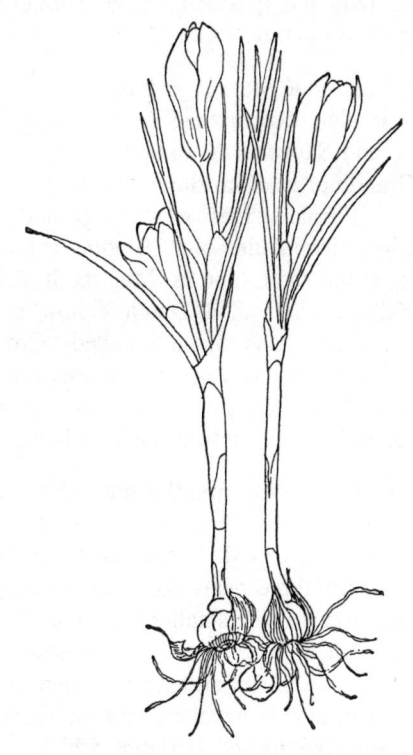

Crocuses in bloom. New corms are beginning to form on top of the old ones. Short pale sheathing leaves enclose the new corm, the long green leaves, and the flower tubes. They will wither, and their dry, brown bases form the new tunic or wrapping for the young corms.

Crocuses in their native lands may be found in bloom, according to kind, from early autumn until mid-spring. I am dividing them into spring- and fall-flowering species for easier consideration, covering the spring-flowering ones here, the others in Chapter IX.

DUTCH CROCUSES. These garden varieties, developed from the wild ones, are best known and most widely grown. They are larger and taller than the species crocuses (about six inches). Most are varieties of *Crocus vernus*.

Enchantress. Lilac-blue, darker at base.
Excelsior. Lilac-blue, deeper than 'Enchantress.'
Jeanne d'Arc and Snowstorm. Pure white.
Purpureus Grandiflorus. Rich dark blue-purple.
Striped Beauty. Purple stripes on white ground.
Vanguard. Light silvery lilac-blue. Blooms earlier than other *vernus* varieties, at the same time as 'Mammoth Yellow.'
Mammoth Yellow. Also called 'Dutch Yellow' or 'Large Yellow,' is a garden flower also wrongly called "Crocus aureus," "luteus," and "flavus." It has been in gardens for at least two hundred years, and its wild antecedents are not known. It is vigorous, sterile, and blooms before *vernus* varieties.

SPECIES CROCUSES. These are the ones that appeal to the collector's instinct. They are fine hobby flowers for the small place, even the city back yard. Some like to grow them from seed. It takes at least three years for them to reach blooming size. The species crocuses are smaller than the Dutch crocuses. In spite of their frail appearance, they can stand much harsh weather. They open, often flat and starry, when the sun shines, and close up tight in cloudy weather, rain, or snow.

There are many fine named varieties which are associated with their parent species rather than with the Dutch crocuses. We can consider only a few of these little charmers here, according to sequence of bloom.

*Crocus chrysanthus.* Late winter or very early spring. Deep yellow to orange globular flowers with broad rounded tepals, often feathered with brown or purple outside. It is the parent of many delightful varieties ranging from cream to deep mahogany, also a range of blues from pale to deep.

*C. tomasinianus.* The most dependable of the pre-spring crocuses. The flowers are pale lavender. It spreads by seeds and division, and so is well worth establishing.

*C. sieberi.* Later than *chrysanthus,* with lilac flowers and yellow throat.

*C. biflorus.* White to pale lilac, feathered darker on the outside. There is a good garden form called 'Cloth-of-Silver' or 'Scotch Crocus' that is white, striped with purple.

*C. susianus,* Cloth-of-Gold. Bright gold with red-brown markings outside. Very early, dwarf.

USES OF CROCUSES. Perhaps in more than one place there is a sight similar to the one I enjoy near my home every year. In a strip of grass beside a busy road I can see these happy words spelled out in crocuses: "Spring is here!"

Crocuses can be planted at the edge of foundation plantings, under trees, and in all sorts of odd corners. Avoid stiff circles and spotty effects. They cannot thrive in heavy sod, but can be planted where grass is thin, and grass-cutting can be postponed until their foliage ripens.

They may become a problem in the ordinary flower bed, because the corms are apt to be disturbed and damaged during summer gardening. Better to give them a place where they can make a picture on their own, or with other flowering plants.

I have a happy memory of what might be called a brook of the crocus 'Excelsior.' Thousands of violet-purple cups formed the brook, which varied in width as it flowed in a winding, shining stream among six or eight early-flowering shrubs—pale yellow witch-hazels and salmon-pink flowering quince. Crocuses and shrubs made the picture.

The Dutch varieties are splendid for massing, planted two to four inches apart, combined with other garden varieties of bulbs such as early tulips. The species are suited to rock gardens, to the front of shrub borders and foundation plantings.

PESTS. Rodents are the main pest of crocuses, and a very serious one. Try coarse gravel mixed in the soil over the corms, and be sure to protect them when they are newly planted and the ground is still soft. Methods of rodent control given in Chapter II may be helpful. However, if you have to choose between crocuses and chipmunks, maybe you will enjoy the sight of the little fellows with their tails in the air enough to make up for the loss of some crocus corms. We have squirrels, chipmunks, and rabbits aplenty, and although they do destroy many corms, we still manage to have a few.

## THE LESS PREDICTABLE SMALL BULBS

The following small bulbs are generally less adaptable than the ones already listed. A more thoughtful approach to meeting their specialized requirements is needed. They are given here more or less in the order of garden desirability, based on the ease with which they can be grown.

WINTER-ACONITE (*Eranthis*). About six species of small tuberous-rooted plants belonging to the Buttercup Family, native to Europe and Asia.

Many people complain of failure in trying to establish winter-aconite. This is because the little tubers become drier, harder, and deader the longer they are kept out of the ground. They should be bought as early as possible in the fall, soaked for twenty-four hours, and planted immediately in damp ground. Keep the ground moist after planting. We have planted winter-aconite several times in sun-baked situations as well as partially shaded ones with complete success, but thin woodland or similar

Winter-aconite grows from a brown, irregularly shaped tuber. A lacy green leaf grows directly under each golden flower like a collar.

partly shaded locations where seedlings can grow undisturbed are best for long life and increase.

*Eranthis hyemalis.* Companion to snowdrops. In the Philadelphia region, a few old plantings have so spread through a century or more that those who know where they are make yearly trips to see their extensive golden carpets. The yellow flowers are like large buttercups, each one topping a stem about 4 inches high. The single leaf, directly underneath the flower, is cut into segments and encircles the stem, giving the effect of an Elizabethan ruff.

*E. tubergenii.* Hybrid of *E. hyemalis* and *E. cilicica.* This blooms a little later, and being sterile, the flowers last well. 'Guinea Gold' is a selection with deep yellow flowers and a tinge of bronze in the foliage.

Once established, the fertile *E. hyemalis* seeds itself freely. All sorts increase by extension of the tuberous roots. A patch of winter-aconite is noticeably fragrant, with a strong honey scent that brings bees flocking to it on the first warm sunny days.

Plant the small tubers three to six inches apart, depending on how immediate an effect is wanted. Cover two to three inches.

ANEMONE or WINDFLOWER (*Anemone*). About a hundred species of plants belonging to the Buttercup Family, mostly of the north temperate zone. Those with tuberous rootstocks can be marketed like bulbs.

Those listed here are valued for their bright early bloom. Since they will not withstand very cold weather, a loose mulch —a covering of half-rotted leaves or compost—is advisable the first year at least. The flowers open only in sunlight; foliage is lacy.

*Anemone appenina.* From the woodlands of South Europe. The bright blue flowers, about 1½ inches across, are borne on leafy stems about 6 inches high. It will grow in thin woodlands in association with rhododendrons and azaleas, seeding itself. There are pink, white, and double forms.

*A. blanda.* This blooms a little earlier, with flowers a little larger on slightly shorter stems. It prefers sun, at least in spring. North of Philadelphia, it must have a sheltered location. There are a number of named varieties in variations of blue as well as pink and white forms. It grows on the mountains of Greece.

*A. fulgens,* Flame Anemone. Probably a hybrid species. A little more tender, but it seeds itself freely in the milder regions. Since it is apt to be in full leaf before winter, the shelter of a wall, bank, or hedge on the northerly side is advisable. The brilliant scarlet flowers with black stamens are over two inches across on stems to a foot high. It comes from southern France.

IRIS (*Iris*). Of the approximately 150 species at present included in this genus of the Iris Family, some are bulbous.

Bulbs ready for planting. Darwin tulips on upper left contrast with small bulbs of *Tulipa clusiana*. On top right are daffodil bulbs, and below them are hyacinths on the left, *Scilla sibirica* on the right. Crocus corms in lower center, more tulips at lower left.

Garden flowers which bloom in mid-April. Top left: summer snowflake; top center: daffodil 'Dick Wellband'; top right: a jonquil variety. Bottom left and right: daffodil 'W. P. Milner'; bottom center: Dutch hyacinths and the lower, smaller clusters of grape-hyacinths.

Glory-of-the-snow (*Chionodoxa gigantea*) has bright violet-blue flowers not quite two inches across.

*Right. Scilla sibirica* 'Spring Beauty' hangs blue-violet flowers half bell, half star, on 8-inch stems.

Spring star-flower (*Ipheion uniflorum*) opens its pale lavender stars under a large crape-myrtle shrub.

The summer snowflake produces several green-tipped flowers atop two-foot scapes, while the shorter spring snowflake has but one or sometimes two yellow-tipped flowers.

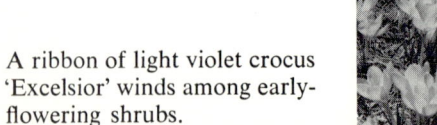

A ribbon of light violet crocus 'Excelsior' winds among early-flowering shrubs.

Among them are a few that bloom very early. Those listed here have four-angled leaves and flowers borne singly on very short stems.

*Iris danfordiae.* This 4-inch-high, soft bright yellow charmer is very early, blooming with the squills. Luckily it is very inexpensive, for it may not bloom after the first year, though some small splits from the bulbs may give a flower now and then.

*I. histrioides major.* This one is more expensive, but such a wonderful blue! Actually, a check with a color chart (the Nickerson Color Fan) shows it to be a brilliant purplish blue, like so many of the so-called blues we have in garden flowers. It usually blooms with the squills. In our garden, it has always petered out in two or three years, but sometimes spots can be found with good summer sun and very good drainage where it will show a little increase.

*I. reticulata.* This one blooms slightly later, with deep violet fragrant flowers which reach a height of 6 inches. In spots it likes it increases into substantial clumps. It grows very well here on a rather steep slope with good afternoon sun. The color is one that must be enjoyed at close range, for it does not carry far. It is easily procured and inexpensive. More expensive and scarcer in American markets are the many varieties in blues and violets. Two very fine ones are 'Cantab,' a lovely light blue, perhaps a hybrid with *I. histrioides,* and 'Harmony,' a medium deep blue.

These small irises need very good drainage indeed, and the bulbs like a summer baking. Severe weather does not hurt the frail-looking flowers, which even withstand strong winds well. *I. reticulata,* which does so well for us, cannot always be counted on, but is the most reliable of the group.

SPRING STAR-FLOWER. Catalogued as *Brodiaea uniflora* or *Tritelia uniflora.* After being switched around among half a dozen genera, this small tunicated bulb is now consigned to

*Ipheion,* a genus of about twelve species, native to South America, belonging to the Amaryllis Family.

*Ipheion uniflorum.* Starry flowers about an inch across, white, tinged blue, one topping each 7-inch scape. In March it often stars lawns in the middle South, where it is sometimes called star-of-Bethlehem. In the Philadelphia area it blooms in April in the protection of a wall or slope. It will grow in favored spots in the New York area. The low, narrow leaves appear in autumn, and can stand more cold than the hidden flower buds, for the plant often survives but does not bloom. It grows into thick clumps which must be divided. Forms of more pronounced lavender-blue are sometimes offered.

FRITILLARIES (*Fritillaria*). Approximately a hundred species comprise a varied group of bulbous plants with leafy stems and nodding bell-shaped flowers, belonging to the Lily Family, and closely related to the genus *Lilium.* They are natives of Europe, Asia, and our own West. The bulbs are non-tunicated, usually composed of but a few thickened, fleshy scales. The gardener is lucky who can find a spot which pleases the fritillaries enough to get a good stand of any of them. The bulbs, like lily bulbs, are easily damaged by becoming too dry, and should be planted promptly in moist soil. It is also possible that they are afflicted by viruses that tend to become widespread in stocks of cultivated plants.

*Fritillaria camtschatcensis.* Native to the northwest coast of North America and to the extreme northeast part of Asia. The flowers are dark maroon, one to three to a stem up to 18 inches tall. This plant is apparently able to persist in soil that does not dry out and with light shade.

*F. imperialis,* Crown Imperial. That curious and elegant plant featured in so many of the Dutch flower paintings. At the top of a leafy stem 2 to 4 feet high there is a cluster of pendulous two-inch bells, yellow, orange, or red. Above the bells rises a topknot of green leaves. The bulbs are large (almost the size of a tennis ball), rather expensive, and have an odor similar to that of a skunk. They should be planted at once in deep, rich, well-drained soil, covered four inches.

Good air circulation will help them to escape botrytis blight. They may be subject to the same fusarium which attacks lily bulbs. At any rate, they used to be grown more extensively than they are now, and were considered rather permanent. They are worth trying once, just for the pleasure of seeing them, and they may flourish for several years. The section of the lily chapter on culture and diseases might well be considered in relation to this interesting plant. Protection from late frosts and from hot afternoon sun should be considered in choosing a site for it.

*F. meleagris,* Guinea-Hen Flower, Checkered-Lily, Snake's-Head. The most dependable of the genus. The bells, rather square across the top, and checkered in rather somber shades of purple, are about 1½ inches long, one to three on a slender stem, 8 to 10 inches high, which also bears a few leaves. *Alba,* a lovely white form veined with green, is very pretty with grape-hyacinths. There are named varieties covering the range from deep purple to white.

The checkered-lilies cannot be counted on for a mass show. They are for odd corners that are a little shady and damp, yet well drained and rich in leaf mold. Not all the bulbs planted are likely to appear and bloom. But it is worthwhile to experiment with a few.

ADDER'S-TONGUE, DOGTOOTH-VIOLET, TROUT-LILY (*Erythronium*). A genus of the Lily Family containing about fifteen North American species and one Eurasian. They are cormous, with dainty drooping flowers like small lilies of the Turkscap shape. They are borne one to several to a stem, which has also two or more leaves near the base. The leaves are wide enough to be an ornamental part of many of the species, because of their beautiful marbling or mottling.

They should be planted immediately in moist ground, and not

allowed to dry out, for they are for the most part flowers of the mountains, blooming as the snows melt. They need cool, humus-rich ground, with light or partial shade. Place a small stone under each corm when planting to keep it from burying itself deeper, and cover with three inches of soil. A sifting of leaf mold now and then is to this plant's liking.

Like the fritillaries, these are flowers for the secluded corner, where they may be grown with other choice plants that will not elbow them out of the way. In a special little garden where I have known them best they flourished with trilliums, some primulas, the delicate *Iris gracilipes,* and *Shortia galacifolia.*

*Erythronium californicum.* Two to three creamy-white flowers to a stem, to a foot high. The dark green leaves are strongly mottled.

*E. grandiflorum,* Glacier-Lily. One to three yellow flowers on stems reaching 10 inches. The leaves are unmottled dark green.

*E. hendersonii.* Several lilac flowers to a stem, to 12 inches high. The leaves are mottled.

*E. revolutum.* One or more white to pink flowers to a stem, to 12 inches high. There are several color forms. The leaves are mottled.

CYCLAMEN. The hardy species are included in Chapter IX.

CHAPTER IV

# Hyacinths

Fragrance is one of the most precious attributes of the common garden hyacinths, and even if only a few are planted, they should be within nose distance of frequently used parts of the property, such as the front door or walk. These are highly civilized plants for the neatly groomed parts of the garden. Not for them the woodland path or the rock garden. They bloom too early for the large border which must give its main display during the warmer months. They will be lost in the expanse unless there are a great many of them. But concentrated in a small garden they are ideal for giving spring an early start. For solid-color formal-bedding effects they are superb. They can also be planted in groups of five or six to give a special color accent among other early flowers.

If only a few hyacinths are planted, the color effect can be emphasized and extended by interplanting with pansies or English daisies of nearly the same color. The contrast of foliage and flower form adds charm.

Hyacinths are lovely companions for the pale pink weeping cherry and other varieties of the early-flowering *Prunus subhirtella. Rhododendron mucronulatum,* which looks like an early azalea in rosy magenta, or its selected pink varieties, such as 'Cornell Pink,' is also a good partner for hyacinths. Other possible companions are forsythia, flowering peaches, flowering quinces, the pure white shrub cherry *Prunus tomentosa;* also andromeda (*Pieris japonica*), the pale yellow *Corylopsis,* and dainty white *Spiraea thunbergii* and *S. arguta.*

## SPECIES HYACINTHS

The genus *Hyacinthus,* belonging to the Lily Family, contains one species which has been of great importance to horticulture as the parent of the well-known garden varieties. There has been some shifting lately of some species into other genera, but for horticultural purposes, they are still called hyacinths here, as they are in catalogs. The thirty species which have been included under this name are native to the lands around the Mediterranean and to tropical and southern Africa. The gay offspring of *H. orientalis* of Greece and the Near East are the important garden group.

*Hyacinthus orientalis,* Common Hyacinth. The wild plant sends up a scape about a foot high hung with fifteen or twenty rather starry bluish-lavender flowers. Knowledgeable gardeners value it for its grace and fragrance, and use it for naturalizing. In many places of moderate climate it persists well. It does not seem to be listed in catalogs, and begging or swapping with one who has it seems to be the way to acquire it.

The variety *albulus* is white, earlier and smaller, from the region of the French-Italian border. It is the ancestor of the Roman hyacinths, forced for early flowers. The white is the prettiest, but there are also pink and blue forms. They should be worth trying outdoors in mild regions south of Philadelphia. I used to plant the white one in northern New Jersey to bloom with other very early bulbs. It would peter out after one spring, because it came up so early the second spring that it could not withstand the cold.

*H. amethystinus* (*Brimeura amethystina*). In early spring it produces spikes 6 to 8 inches high of light lavender-blue drooping flowers, rather tubular, but partially opening into stars. There is a white form.

*H. azureus* (*Hyacinthella azurea;* "Muscari azureum" of catalogs). A small bulb discussed with *Muscari* in Chapter III.

## DUTCH HYACINTHS

In the varieties of *Hyacinthus orientalis* we have the result of generations of effort by Dutch bulb growers, who have produced bulbs that send forth robust stalks a foot or more high, thickly set with starry flowers about an inch across.

The pure light pinks and violet-blues, the deeper shades in rose to deep blues and violets, are especially valuable for spring pictures. Whites and yellows are more abundant among the other spring bulbs, but these are welcome in hyacinths too. Some of the reds are prone to have a touch of harshness, and may detract from the beauty of more delicate colors.

## CULTURE

Hyacinths require very good drainage, and thrive best in a rather light but rich soil. They deteriorate in a few years in heavy soils, and poor, heavy soils that do not drain rapidly may cause the bulbs to rot. They need good sun for part of each day. Plants that are stunted or look unhealthy should be removed, bulbs and all.

Bulbs are often offered in several sizes for the same varieties. The top sizes are used for forcing. The third size, called the bedding size, is the one to use for outdoor planting. The lighter spikes are better able to withstand rain and wind. For home forcing, the first- and second-size bulbs will please most people as much as or more than the exhibition size, which is largest of all.

The first spring after planting, even the bedding size will give fat, well-filled flower stalks. In springs following, these are sparser, and two or more stalks may take the place of one. But after two or three years, except in the best sites, the bulbs gradually disappear, except for an odd one here and there that seems to have found a spot especially favorable.

The bulbs are covered with three inches of soil when the soil is heavy; to five inches when the soil is fairly light. They look best in groups of several of a kind. It is also pleasing to see two values—a light and a dark—of the same color together.

For formal bedding effects, they must be planted at uniform depth for uniform bloom. If more than one variety is to be used, they should be kinds that will bloom together. Plant all bulbs the same distance apart (six to eight inches) for a solid effect, and stagger the rows.

After their flowering, if the space is wanted for other plants immediately, the hyacinths can be dug and heeled-in for ripening and stored until fall. Heeling-in consists of digging a shallow trench, placing the bulbs in it, and throwing the soil back over them. The foliage, of course, is out in the open. It is, in effect, a sort of temporary planting which allows the foliage to continue its food-making function. It is not necessary for the plants to be upright, and they are often placed on their sides or at an angle.

Only the largest of the bulbs will be satisfactory for replanting for a solid effect. New ones will be required to make up the number needed. The smaller bulbs can be planted in other places where their color will be attractive, but top size is not needed.

## VARIETIES OF DUTCH HYACINTHS

**WHITE**
  *Arentine Arendsen. Early. Narrow spike.
  Carnegie. Late. Compact spike.
  *L'Innocence. Very popular. Large bells.
  Nevada. A newer white.
YELLOW TO SALMON, listed from light to dark
  City of Haarlem. Creamy yellow.
  *Prince Henry. Pale yellow.

  * forcing varieties

Moonlight. Pale yellow.
Yellow Hammer. Golden yellow.
*Orange Boven (Salmonette). Rather small orange salmon.

LIGHT PINK
*Crown Princess Margaret. Large spike.
*Lady Derby. Similar in color to 'Crown Princess Margaret.' For late forcing.
*Anne Marie. Early. A soft pink which changes to salmon pink.
Gypsy Queen. Salmon rose.

MEDIUM PINK
*Gertrude. Compact spike. For outdoors and late forcing.
*Princess Irene. Early soft pink. Forces early.

DEEP PINK
*Pink Pearl. Good for early forcing.
*Queen of the Pinks. For late forcing; good garden variety.

RED
Cyclops. Very bright red; if planted too near pale pinks, apt to make them look insipid.
*Jan Bos. Similar very bright red. Early.
*La Victoire. Early. Rose red that looks well with lighter pinks.
*Tubergen's Scarlet. Deep bright red.

LIGHT BLUE (There are no true blues. All have a touch of violet.)
Côte d'Azur. Nearest to true blue.
*Myosotis. Early. Good indoors and out.
*Perle Brillante. Later; similar color.

MEDIUM BLUE
*King of the Blues. Late. Good indoors and out.
*Ostara. Early. Good indoors and out.

LILAC TO PURPLE AND VIOLET
General Eisenhower. Very deep blue-purple.
*Grand Maître. Deep lavender. Early, good indoors and out.
*Marie. Early dark blue-purple.
Purple King. Mauve purple. Late.
Viola. Deep violet.

\* forcing varieties

CHAPTER V

# Daffodils

Daffodils are flowers of animation and grace, turning their faces to the sun, bowing away from the wind. Their beauty, combined with their ability to prosper and increase, often under neglect, wins them high regard. They become heirlooms, and are shared with friends.

In the reign of Queen Elizabeth, as many as twenty-four kinds were being grown in London gardens. But it was not until the nineteenth century that gardeners began to breed and select them for better garden flowers. Many fine, vigorous varieties have originated in the Netherlands, but most of the daffodil varieties have come into being in the British Isles. Australia, New Zealand, and the United States are now contributing their share. About 9,500 names appear in the 1961 register issued by the Royal Horticultural Society. More than 4,000 names of obsolete varieties were dropped from the 1955 list. Of course only a portion of those 9,500 varieties are obtainable, which is fortunate. It is hard enough as it is to choose among so many.

Daffodils belong to the Amaryllis Family. They form a complex and dynamic genus, *Narcissus,* containing some forty-odd species. There are many subspecies and wild varieties, as well as wild hybrids, resulting in an intricate and fascinating maze of names and synonyms for those who care to investigate it. During the centuries these wild plants have been brought into gardens, and the garden progeny have further complicated the botanical picture, for who can now say, of many, which is wilding and which is garden child?

In the wild, daffodils range from western Europe (Sweden, England, and Portugal) down through Switzerland, sweeping along through Greece, rimming the whole Mediterranean, sending fingers into Africa. From the eastern shores of the Mediterranean they cross through Asia to China and Japan. Although they arrived on the American continent only with the white settlers, so well have they taken to their new homes that they survive, flourish, and spread even when the houses around which they were planted have disappeared.

Wild daffodils, according to kind, range from about 3 to 20 inches in height, and from hardy to tender. Some bear but one flower to a scape, some several. The flowers vary from about one to two inches in width, and in length (seen in profile) from almost flat to over an inch. The color range is narrow, from yellow into white and white with a red eye. The daffodil species which comprise the Jonquil Section and the variations of *Narcissus tazetta* (one of them the well-known "Paper-White"), are notable for their fragrance.

Generations of breeding and selection have shuffled the shapes and colors, and coaxed the red to dilute into near-pink. We now have larger flowers with broader tepals. Even more important, the fine modern varieties are *tetraploids*. This means that they have double the number of chromosomes of most of the older varieties, which are *diploids*. The well-known snapdragons called "Tetrasnaps" are a demonstration of what chromosome-doubling does for a plant: it gives stronger stems, thicker flower substance, and greater vigor. The modern daffodils, therefore, give a range of flowers of greater garden value, although the wild species and many of the old-time varieties are still esteemed.

## GENERAL CULTURE

Daffodils grow well in the kind of reasonably good soil that is needed to make any home grounds attractive. They may be grown in full sun or partial or light shade. They will grow in ground covers and in grass. Those who want to win blue ribbons with them will give them very special culture, but those who grow them to adorn their spring gardens care more about diversity and an abundance of flowers for as long a season as possible.

Ideally, the soil for daffodils should be fertile and mellow to a depth of eighteen inches, but a foot of good well-drained soil will give satisfactory flowers. This allows the bulbs to be covered with four inches of soil, and leaves several inches under them for their large masses of roots. Dig the soil and work it over well to a good depth before planting your bulbs. Daffodil experts do not use manure, fresh or old, where it may come in contact with the bulbs. Many do not use it at all, especially in regions with hot summers. Where soils keep cool, in the North, or in shade, processed manures are probably perfectly safe, but they should be dug in and thoroughly mixed some time before planting is done. Other forms of humus, especially peat moss, can be used, and for plant food a fertilizer low in nitrogen can be mixed in.

New bulbs should be planted as early in the fall as they can be obtained, usually in September or early October. Delay in planting may mean the loss of some of the bulbs, which may go soft while they are kept out of the ground.

In stony or heavy ground it may be possible to cover the bulbs with only three inches of soil. They will probably need resetting in a few years, as the bloom will start to decrease sooner than if they can be set a little deeper. Small daffodils with small bulbs are set two or three inches deep. They are discussed later in this chapter.

In planning planting distances, gardeners must choose between immediate and long-term effects. Daffodils increase so that bulbs planted six inches apart will grow into a solid mass in three or four years, and will need to be taken up and divided. For a longer span between dividing, eight to ten inches between bulbs is satisfactory. In naturalizing, a foot apart is satisfactory.

WINTER CARE. In cold regions, winter mulches may be found advisable. The mulch, of material that will not become waterlogged and packed, should be put on after the top layer of soil has frozen, and unless it is a kind that can be left on as a summer mulch, should be removed as soon as spring growth starts.

SPRING AND SUMMER CARE. When they are in beds where cultivation is possible, the daffodils benefit by shallow cultivation to keep the soil receptive to rain and to destroy young weeds. For flowers of extra quality, a light sprinkling of fertilizer can be scratched in around the bulbs. Choose one low in nitrogen, or use one without any nitrogen at all. However, this extra feeding is not a yearly necessity, especially in soil that was well prepared at the start.

Enthusiasts snap off the heads of faded flowers, both to improve the garden's appearance and to save the bulb the work of making seed, if by chance any has been set. The green scape acts like a leaf and need not be removed. However, not enough seed is set in the average garden to make flower removal important except for aesthetic reasons.

Since full functioning of the foliage gives the best flowers, leaves must be allowed to complete their cycle. At first they stand upright, but as the weeks go by, they flop over. Some gardeners gather them into bunches, double them over, and slip an elastic or tie a string around them. If this is not done until they reach the limp stage, probably it does not do any great harm, as long as they are tied only loosely. However, it is obvious that they do not receive the light they would if left alone.

It seems better to place the daffodils in back of the later-flowering plants that will hide the early stages of foliage ripening. Annuals can be set near them as soon as the weather allows, and the leaves, as they become limp, simply pushed over to the side. When the leaves have withered, they should be removed, and soil scratched over the holes to discourage daffodil flies from crawling down to lay their eggs on the necks of the bulbs.

Mulches during the blooming season protect the flowers from mud splashes, maintain even moisture and temperature conditions in the soil, and save the labor of cultivating. (A few weeds may need hand pulling.) We have used hardwood sawdust very successfully. It was put on about three inches thick. Never have we had finer flowers, with vigorous growth and wonderful bloom for many years, without lifting the bulbs. It is supposed to be wise to add fertilizer when sawdust is used, for sawdust may rob the soil of nitrogen as it decays. Premature yellowing of the leaves would be a sign that fertilizer is needed. Coarse pine needles, buckwheat hulls, and cocoa hulls make good mulches. Wood chips and material of similar coarseness are apt to impede leaf growth in spring, causing distortion.

CUTTING FLOWERS FOR THE HOUSE. Who can resist picking a few? But be careful of foliage, especially on bulbs blooming for the first time. Take a leaf here, another there, preferably from well-established older clumps. Save them if you can from one batch of cut flowers to the next.

DIVIDING AND REPLANTING DAFFODILS. A patch of daffodils may make a wonderful display of bloom one spring and hardly any the next. Or the decline of bloom may be gradual. Less bloom is the signal for dividing and resetting, but the wise gardener forestalls this condition by digging up the plants before it takes place. If the bulbs reach the point of little or no bloom, it may take two or three years after resetting to bring them back to good performance. The closeness of growth is an obvious symptom of overcrowding. Often the foliage and flowers fall over easily, and sometimes the flower buds blast, withering without opening.

Varieties differ in the length of time they can go without

dividing. Cultural conditions make a difference, too. The gardener must treat each clump according to its appearance.

The daffodils are best dug after blooming, when the foliage has reached the yellow stage of the ripening process. Near Philadelphia, this is in late June. Digging with a fork is a little safer than digging with a spade, but care must still be taken not to slice through the bulbs.

Shake off the excess earth, and pull the clump apart gently. Do not break apart bulbs that are not ready to separate of their own accord. A good hosing helps to clean off the soil, but the bulbs should be well dried afterward. Keep a label with each clump, and separate the varieties.

The bulbs should be spread for further drying in a shady, airy place. It may take several days for the foliage to reach the stage when it can be pulled easily from the bulbs. Unless the variety is especially valued, the smallest bulbs can be discarded. Throw away any damaged or unhealthy-looking bulbs.

When the bulbs are free of any moist appearance on the outside, they can be stored in shallow boxes or loose-meshed bags. Old nylon stockings make good bulb bags. During the summer the bulbs should be in a place where they will have access to plenty of air in a cool, dry location.

Replanting can be done in late August or September, when the sun has lost some of its punch and soils are cooling. Inspect the bulbs as planting goes on, and discard any that are soft, especially at the base.

EARLY TRANSPLANTING AND SOIL TEMPERATURES. It is also possible to transplant a clump of daffodils when it is in bloom, although this is less desirable from the point of view of culture. The clump must be lifted carefully to preserve the roots as fully as possible, replanted immediately, and well watered. If dividing is needed, do it after the foliage has ripened.

Bulbs may be replanted, after lifting, cleaning, and drying, without the summer storage period. Where summers are cool, or the bulbs are to go into a place with summer shade, this method may be satisfactory. In warm soils, losses from basal rot may result. A summer in dry storage allows for the healing of small injuries, but when bulbs are replanted right away, rot organisms can attack through these wounds.

Bulbs may also be dug while the foliage is still green, and heeled-in (*see* Glossary) in an out-of-the-way place until the foliage ripens. The bulbs are then cleaned, divided, dried, and stored.

## DISEASES AND PESTS

Daffodils may be grown for years without a thought of pests. Rodents do not bother them. However, it is well to be aware of possible problems.

VIRUS DISEASES. There are several that vary in their effect on the health of the plants. Leaves which develop brown tips early in the season, silvery streaks in the leaves, chocolate spots, and yellow striping or mottling are symptoms to look for. Plants on which the foliage withers away especially early after flowering in spite of sufficient moisture are also suspect.

Yellow stripe and mosaic are the two viruses commonly encountered. Yellow stripe shows up early in the year, and is easier to detect when the leaves are only a few inches high. One bad leaf on a plant can be ignored. But if several leaves on a plant show striping, it should be removed promptly. In some varieties, stripe causes dwarfing and lack of bloom; in others, growth and bloom are little affected. The striping is often not clearly defined, but observant gardeners can learn to detect it very quickly if they once have a chance to observe it among their plants. The pale yellow mottling caused by mosaic becomes apparent later in the season after flowering.

Viruses cannot be cured. Plants should be removed promptly, for the diseases are spread by aphids. The soil is not contaminated, and it is safe to plant new bulbs in the same place. It is poor economy to spare even an expensive bulb. If only one bulb in a clump is infected, the foliage can be cut off. The bulb, left in place, is destroyed by carefully dropping a little oil mixed with 2, 4-D (one part of weed killer to five parts of oil) between the bases of the leaves. Check the clump carefully the next spring to be sure there is no sign of disease in the remaining bulbs.

BASAL ROT. This fungus disease is associated with hot soils and poor drainage, and hot storage conditions. It is more of a problem in places of sustained summer heat than where summers are cool. To avoid it, Southern fanciers depend on peat moss for humus instead of compost and manure. They use chemical fertilizers low in nitrogen. Where basal rot is common, it should be watched for whenever the bulbs are handled. It begins as a softening of the area around the basal plate, and often spreads through the interior of the bulb without becoming visible. Or it may be seen as a discolored patch at the basal plate. Pressure at the base of the bulb often discloses its presence. Slightly diseased bulbs that are planted send up poor, stunted growth, and should be taken out and destroyed at once.

Basal rot may develop in bulbs in transit. Bulbs should be pressed at the edge of the basal plate for signs of softness, preferably when the bags are opened on arrival, certainly at planting time. Two checks are better than one. The basal rot fungus can live in the soil, so do not plant daffodils again for several years in a spot where bulbs have rotted.

If basal rot has been present in the garden, or if you have had bulbs go soft or dry and powdery during storage, soaking the bulbs in a fungicide at the time they are dug for dividing is very helpful. Discard any damaged bulbs, and those showing any signs of mold or rot, and treat the rest. One method is to immerse them in rubbing alcohol for ten minutes after they have been cleaned and divided. Another is to soak them in a solution of Mersolite-W. One plastic teaspoon of Mersolite is mixed into a paste with hot water, then added to five gallons of cold water in a non-metallic container. Use a stick for stirring to keep the material diffused through the water. Wear rubber gloves. The bulbs to be dipped are placed in bags of loose mesh or old stockings, and submerged for five minutes. They are then well dried and stored. Some people dip them again before planting. Dispose of the Mersolite carefully, using large quantities of water to dilute it further. Mersolite-W comes in four-ounce jars and lasts a long time since so little is used. It is a mercury compound, and metal surfaces absorb mercury; hence the need to avoid the use of metal in all stages of the treatment. It is also poisonous, and should not be allowed to come in contact with the skin.

There is a precautionary treatment of bulbs. They may be coated with a fungicidal powder such as Ceresan, Semesan, Arasan, or Spergon. Shake a little into a paper bag with the bulbs and turn the bag about until the bulbs are coated. Wear gloves when handling the bulbs, and be careful not to inhale the dust.

DAFFODIL FLY. This insect may cause losses from time to time, but unless damage is serious, may not even be noticed. The fly is about ½ inch long, fuzzy, and may be banded in various patterns of red, yellow, black, and white, or just brown or black. It resembles a small bumblebee, but does not act like one. It is sluggish in cold and wet, avoids shade and wind. In poor weather it can often be caught while resting on daffodil leaves. In warmth it darts up and away if disturbed. It darts rapidly from place to place, zigzagging among the daffodil leaves. Its wings often make a whining noise.

The flies emerge from the bulbs at flowering time and are active for about six weeks. They lay their eggs on the leaves at ground level, or on the ground near them. Or they may crawl down the holes left by the withering leaves and lay the eggs directly on the necks of the bulbs. The young maggot bores into the bulb and eats out the inside. Usually there is just one to a bulb, but there may be two or three.

Bee-like insects showing an undue interest in your daffodils should be suspected. Flies have but one pair of wings, and bees have two pairs, so it is only necessary to catch a few and examine them to find out whether there is an infestation.

If there is, chlordane, aldrin, or heptachlor may be used around the bulbs in planting (bulbs can be dusted with 25% dieldrin before planting). The granular forms are less dusty than the powders. These are all deadly poisons. Inhaling the dust is extremely hazardous. Chlordane and dieldrin can be absorbed through the skin. They are poisonous to birds, pets, and children as well as the gardener.

Prudent people may prefer safer methods. If you have daffodil flies, acquire a butterfly net and learn to catch them, or set up a bounty system for the children. Keep the soil close around the foliage as it withers, finally remove and burn it, and rake over the holes that are left.

The lesser daffodil-fly maggots feed in bulbs already injured and containing rotten tissue. Twenty or thirty may be found in a bulb. They are often found in iris rhizomes following rot, and are considered scavengers. The adults are about two-thirds the length of the large fly, with much less hair in light bands.

But there are also *useful* hover flies which resemble daffodil flies, and act much the same way. Both the adults and the larvae feed on aphids and other insects. So if you are suspicious of the flies in your garden, take the time to check on their activities. When you dig out plants that are behaving badly, examine them to see if they have been damaged by the flies. If flies are indeed bothering your bulbs, it is well to go after them, even if it means destroying some useful insects.

NEMATODES. The *bulb and stem nematode* causes deformities in the leaves called *spikkels*. These are blistered areas that can be felt by running the leaf between thumb and forefinger. Leaves may be curled and twisted. As spring progresses, the spikkels may turn brown. These are not the little ripples in the leaves which sometimes appear when the plant is otherwise perfectly healthy in appearance. The bulbs of infested plants develop brown areas which appear as brown rings if the bulb is cut in half. This nematode also attacks other bulbs and perennials, including tulips, scillas, phlox, and campanulas. Fortunately, there are different strains, and each sticks to its particular favorite.

The *root lesion nematode* attacks many plants, including common weeds. When daffodils are lifted for division, the nematode does not survive in the bulb, but dies as the roots dry. When bulbs are infested, it is at the root. Examination shows roots rotted off, but an otherwise healthy-looking bulb. Growth, of course, is stunted. Treatment of ground infested with this nematode involves procedures to be undertaken by an expert. If you have good reason to suspect nematodes, consult your county agent. These pests are the subject of a great deal of study, and better approaches to their control can be expected.

If this account of pests and diseases sounds appalling, remember that you may never have any of them in your garden. Commercial growers now know how to control nematodes, and try to keep their bulb stocks clean of other troubles. They succeed wonderfully well most of the time. Removal and destruction of suspicious-looking bulbs are important in the garden routine. Knowledge of some of the troubles you could have is a useful tool.

## CHOOSING DAFFODILS FOR THE GARDEN

In choosing daffodils for garden adornment, try for a range of shapes and colors which will give as long a season as possible. In general, the first daffodils to bloom are yellow, with trumpets or large cups, and the late ones are white, with cups reduced to eyes that may be white, orange, or red. Midway in the daffodil season there is a tremendous group of large-cupped flowers with white perianths and color in the cups.

Early whites and late yellows, then, extend the interest of the season. The first small cups are welcome; the last trumpets, treasured.

Jonquils are one group of daffodils, consisting of several species and wild varieties having certain traits in common. Most are quite small, and many are sweetly scented. Those best known in gardens are fragrant, with several small-cupped yellow flowers to a scape. Several forms of jonquils are naturalized in the South. All jonquils are daffodils, but only certain daffodils can be called jonquils. There is further information about them in the lists which follow. *Narcissus* is the botanical name of all the flowers commonly called narcissus, daffodils, and jonquils.

The lists of varieties presented here are drawn up to show as wide a range as possible of shapes and colors through the season. Some of them are standard varieties found in most commercial lists, but for most of them it is necessary to look in the lists of specialists. There are several dealers in the United States who can supply the best and most interesting of daffodil varieties, and ordering them is a perfectly simple procedure.

The lists follow the present classification of the Royal Horticultural Society of Great Britain, devised in 1950 to replace the one in use since 1923. The present one is getting into difficulties as new inter-division hybrids are created, and may be revised in the future. It is used as the basis for describing new varieties as they are introduced, and for daffodil show schedules. Every few years the RHS issues a list of daffodil varieties with the classifications.

Some of the terms of the 1923 classification linger on in catalogs and in the vocabulary of those who have grown daffodils for many years, and so they are explained here:

Incomparabilis ("Incomps")—now in Division II (Large Cups) (a) and (b)

Giant Leedsii—now in Division II (c)

Barrii—Division III (Small Cups) (a) and (b)

Leedsii—Division III (c)

A classification of a group of garden plants is the work of a group of persons whose interest and experience qualify them to undertake the task, and enable the result to gain acceptance from the gardening world. Classifications are useful aids in understanding large groups of garden flowers. Since they are in print, they are necessarily rigid, until, again in print, changes are made as needed. There are always borderline flowers in classifications, and some may waver back and forth over the lines from one season to the next.

Here is the Royal Horticultural Society classification of daffodils:

**Division I. Trumpet Narcissi of Garden Origin**
Distinguishing characters: One flower to a stem; trumpet or corona as long as or longer than the perianth segments.
(a) Perianth colored; corona colored, not paler than the perianth.
(b) Perianth white; corona colored.
(c) Perianth white; corona white, not paler than the perianth.
(d) Any color combination not falling into (a), (b), or (c).

**Division II. Large-Cupped Narcissi of Garden Origin**
Distinguishing characters: One flower to a stem; cup or corona more than one-third but less than equal to the length of the perianth segments.
Subdivisions (a), (b), (c), and (d) as in Division I.

**Division III. Small-Cupped Narcissi of Garden Origin**
Distinguishing characters: One flower to a stem; cup or corona not more than one-third the length of the perianth segments.
Subdivisions (a), (b), (c), and (d) as in Division I.

**Division IV. Double Narcissi of Garden Origin**
Distinguishing character: Double flowers (one or more to a stem)

**Division V. Triandrus Narcissi of Garden Origin**
Distinguishing characters: Characteristics of *N. triandrus* clearly evident.
(a) Cup or corona not less than two-thirds the length of the perianth segments.
(b) Cup or corona less than two-thirds the length of the perianth segments.

**Division VI. Cyclamineus Narcissi of Garden Origin**
Distinguishing characters: Characteristics of *N. cyclamineus* clearly evident.
Subdivisions (a) and (b) as in Division V.
**Division VII. Jonquilla Narcissi of Garden Origin**
Distinguishing characters: Characteristics of any of the *N. jonquilla* group clearly evident.
Subdivisions (a) and (b) as in Division V.
**Division VIII. Tazetta Narcissi of Garden Origin**
Distinguishing characters: Characteristics of any of the *N. tazetta* group clearly evident.
**Division IX. Poeticus Narcissi of Garden Origin**
Distinguishing characters: Characteristics of any of the *N. poeticus* group without any admixture of any other.
**Division X. Species and Wild Forms and Hybrids**
All species and wild, or reputedly wild, forms and hybrids.
**Division XI. Miscellaneous Narcissi**
All narcissi not falling into any of the foregoing divisions.

## DAFFODILS ACCORDING TO CLASSIFICATION

Heights range from about 16 to 25 inches, except where other heights are indicated. Those over 20 inches are called tall; those 16 inches or a little less are called short. Small daffodils are in a separate section of this chapter, and will be found on pages 92 to 95.

**Ia. Colored Trumpets**

All now available are yellow, from very pale to deep gold. There are a few new ones with red or orange in the trumpet, but it will be several years before even the most eager collectors can have them.

EARLY

Grapefruit. Very pale.
*Lord Nelson. Medium yellow; wide trumpet, slight frill.
Moonstruck. Very pale. Narrow gently frilled trumpet.
*Mulatto. Very pale, matures to almost a Id (reverse bicolor).
*Priority. Gold.
*Scotch Gold. Very deep gold, almost orange. Frilled rim.
Tintoretto. Pale; apricot in trumpet.

* earliest

## Hardy Garden Bulbs

EARLY MIDSEASON
*Arctic Gold. Deep gold; tall.
Burgomeester Gouverneur. Large; smooth trumpet.
Garron. Soft lemon; tall.
Insurpassable. Large yellow; tall.
Lemon Meringue. Very pale.
Luna Moth. Very pale; large. Long narrow trumpet.
Ulster Prince. Bright yellow.

MIDSEASON
Counsellor. Medium yellow; slender trumpet.
Cromarty. Deep gold; serrated trumpet.
Goldcourt. Golden.
Hunter's Moon. Clear lemon.
Kingscourt. Medium gold, rather straight trumpet. Fine form.

MID-LATE
Arranmore. Deep golden yellow, tall, rather straight trumpet.
Bastion. Deep gold; long straight trumpet.
Donore. Bright gold.
Slieveboy. Large soft yellow.

**Ib. Bicolor Trumpets**
Perianth white; most with yellow trumpets; a few with pink.

EARLY
*Chula. Creamy yellow trumpet.
Jefta. Free flowering; sturdy.
Mirth. Rich yellow trumpet.
Patria. Long lemon-yellow trumpet.
Trousseau. Soft yellow trumpet turns to cheesy buff. Tall.

EARLY MIDSEASON
Bonnington. Tall, large, good contrast.
Content. Pale greenish-yellow trumpet fades pale, with yellow frill.
Foresight. Clear lemon trumpet.
Frolic. Ruffled rich yellow trumpet.
Lapford. Soft yellow trumpet.
Preamble. Good color contrast.
Zest. Pale yellow trumpet fades to cream.

* earliest

MIDSEASON
  Effective. Good color contrast. Yellow halo in perianth.
  Indiscreet. Small flower; pink trumpet.
**Ic. White Trumpets**
EARLY
  *High Sierra. Tall, large, sturdy.
  Silverdale. Tall, sturdy ivory.
EARLY MIDSEASON
  Beersheba. Long trumpet. Stem a little short, but fine flower.
MIDSEASON
  Cantatrice. Long slender trumpet; well-proportioned refined flower.
  Mount Hood. Wide trumpet.
  Mrs. Ernst H. Krelage. Creamy.
  Rosabella. Palest pink frilled trumpet.
  Vigil. Large, tall, pure white, fine proportions. Good vigorous growth.
LATE
  Rashee. Tall; smoothly rolled rim; medium-sized flower.
  White Tartar. Large and strong.
**Id. Other Color Combinations**
  Reverse bicolors, with trumpets paler than the perianths. A fairly new group, with few varieties. At present, the varieties must be out a few days before the trumpets fade to give the reverse effect. They are attractive, but we can expect better ones in the future.
EARLY
  Entrancement. Opens greenish yellow; trumpet turns nearly white.
EARLY MIDSEASON
  Lunar Sea. Opens pale lemon; trumpet turns white. Tall.
  Nampa. Deep lemon perianth with white halo; trumpet fades white. Tall.
  Spellbinder. Greenish-lemon trumpet fades white.

\* earliest

## IIa. Large Cups. Perianth Colored, Corona Colored

All have yellow perianths. Some have yellow cups (crowns or coronas) and some have orange or red in the cups. Some look like trumpets, but the cups are a little too short to meet the trumpet measurements.

EARLY

Aerolite. Medium yellow. Almost a trumpet.
*Carlton. Soft yellow; broad cup.
Ceylon. Tall; goblet-shaped dark orange-red cup.
*Fortune. Tall. Light orange cup. Prolific and vigorous; a classic.
Galway. Gold; trumpet-like cup.
*Jalna. Earliest red cup. Cup yellow with red edge.

EARLY MIDSEASON

Adventure. Light yellow; cup a little deeper. Almost a trumpet.
Agathon. Large. Smooth straight trumpet cup. Medium yellow.
Armada. Deep yellow perianth, deep orange-red cup.
Foxhunter. Bright yellow perianth; narrow red-orange cup.
Golden Torch. Bright gold; trumpet-like cup.
Home Fires. Tall. Bright yellow perianth; orange-red cup.
Red Ranger. Deep yellow perianth; deep orange-red cup.
Rustom Pasha. Long orange-red cup; tall.
Sun Chariot. Large, tall. Bright gold with large bright orange-red cup.

MIDSEASON

Aranjuez. Rather flat cup banded orange-red.
Carbineer. Tall; orange-red cup.
Castlerock. Deep yellow with crimson-red crown.
Court Martial. Bright yellow; long, deep orange-red crown.
Dunkeld. Wide shallow orange-red cup.
Lemnos. Very pale with shallow bowl-shaped cup.
Narvik. Tall; frilled orange-red crown.

* earliest

Paricutin. Deep gold; large flat fiery red crown. Tall.
St. Egwin. Very tall; soft yellow with short cup.
MID-LATE
Amberley. Soft yellow; bowl-shaped cup.
LATE
*Badger. Orange-red straight-sided cup.
*Kindled. Dark red shallow cup.
Ultimus. Perianth creamy; cup soft orange.

**IIb.  Large Cups. Perianth White, Corona Colored**

This section contains the greatest number of varieties. The color in the cups ranges from gold and yellow to deep red, solid or in different arrangements of bands. Sometimes the cup is white with a delicate rim of color. At present this section contains most of the pinks. These often have buff cups when they open, the pink (which usually contains a tint of yellow) developing a day or so later.

EARLY
Brunswick. Tall; lemon rim.
†Penvose. Cup opens pale yellow, turns buff. Tall.
Promisso. Often pink in cup, but hot weather fades it.
†South Pacific. Starry cup of soft yellow.

EARLY MIDSEASON
Allurement. Broad, fully ruffled crown of apricot pink.
Carnlough. Cup pale citron and pink.
Coverack Perfection. Wide shallow crown, salmon and gold.
John Evelyn. Cup very frilled, pale lemon.
Personality. Smooth, neat, unfrilled lemon crown.
Pink Smiles. Deep amber-pink cup.
Polindra. Clear yellow crown.
Tramore. Trumpet-like bright lemon cup, frilled at rim.
Tunis. Tall; wide frilled crown, all lemon, fading to white with gold edge.
Ulster Beauty. Tall; white trumpet-like crown edged lemon.

\* latest
† earliest

### MIDSEASON

Angeles. Broad, much-ruffled crown with yellow center fading white.

Arbar. Flat orange-red crown.

Buncrana. Frilled peach-orange cup.

Chiffon. Small; pure pink cup.

Daviot. Orange-coral crown rimmed pale yellow.

Elation. Broad ruffled medium-yellow crown.

Greeting. Small lemon cup.

Mabel Taylor. Frilled wide crown banded rose-pink.

Pink Lace. Crown very ruffled, opens pale yellow, turns shell pink.

Radiation. Large crown turns from pale buff to salmon pink.

Rose of Tralee. Long crown flushed rosy apricot pink.

Selma Lagerlöf. Wide ruffled greenish-yellow crown edged apricot orange.

Statue. Clear lemon crown.

Tudor Minstrel. Frilled orange-yellow cup.

Tuskar Light. Wide yellow crown with broad orange-red band.

### MID-LATE

Ann Abbott. Fluted cup edged pink.

Azalea. Flared pink cup, deeper rim.

Ballet. Cup soft pink, deeper rim.

Crown Derby. Gold crown edged red.

Fermoy. Frilled bowl-shaped crown orange-red fading to gold at base.

Hillmount. Dark crimson crown.

Kilworth. Dark orange-red cup.

King Cardinal. Intense red flat crown.

Mrs. R. O. Backhouse. Apricot-pink trumpet-like crown.

Rose Ribbon. Flaring crown with broad band of bright salmon-rose.

### LATE

Alicante. Deep apricot-orange cup.

Killala. Rather small. Yellow crown edged orange-red.
Stability. Pale primrose crown.
Tryst. Small very pale cup.

## IIc. Large Cups, All White

EARLY

Dunfane. Tall. Trumpet-like cup opens pale yellow, turns pure white.
Parkmore. Neat trumpet cup pale turning pure white.
Snow Dream. Crown opens cream, soon turns white.
Truth. Evenly rolled rim, trumpet cup opens white.
White Nile. Medium size. Short cup.

EARLY MIDSEASON

Courage. Large; trumpet-like cup.
Killaloe. Large; widely flaring frilled crown.
Wedding Bell. Bell-shaped crown.
Zero. Vase-shaped crown spreading slightly at mouth. Tall.

MIDSEASON

Ave. Medium-sized but broad crown. Very smooth form.
Cloneen. Tall; cup goblet-shaped.
Easter Moon. Short cup, green inside at base.
Greenland. Medium crown; base green inside.
White Spire. Very tall; shallow crown.

MID-LATE

Nakota. Medium small. Crown creamy, finely frilled.
Olivet. Tall. Bowl-shaped ruffled crown cream fading white.
Sloeblossom. Medium cup, pale cream; perianth very white.
Wedding Gift. Narrow trumpet-like cup. Stands hot climates well.

LATE

Corby. Creamy crown turning white.
Frozen. Pure white.
Pigeon. Rather small, very neat. Medium-length crown.

## IId. Any Other Color Combination (Reverse Bicolors)

Like Id, a new group, still small. Reverse effect does not appear until flowers have been open for a day or so.

EARLY
   Binkie. Opens pale lemon, straight cup turns white.
EARLY MIDSEASON
   Nazareth. Rather small. Opens pale yellow. Perianth develops white halo, cup turns white.
MIDSEASON
   Bethany. Opens yellow. Trumpet cup fades white.
   Cocktail. Opens soft lemon, cup turns white.
   Lemon Doric. Tall; opens lemon; narrow trumpet cup turns white.
MID-LATE
   Daydream. Opens lemon. Trumpet cup fades white.

**IIIa. Small Cups. Yellow Perianth, Cup Yellow, Orange, or Red**

   A small group, but contains a few flowers of quality.
EARLY MIDSEASON
   Ballysillan. Shallow red cup.
   Market Merry. Perianth gold, cup red.
MIDSEASON
   Apricot Distinction. Perianth opens red-apricot, fades in sun. Cup deep orange.
   Chungking. Tall; golden perianth, shallow red cup.
   Danger. Small crinkled red eye.
   Jezebel. Red-gold perianth, deeper cup. Fades in sun.
   Mangosteen. Orange cup.
   Rapallo. Very flat crown, deep gold edged red.
   Therm. Large shallow deep red cup.
   Varna. Shallow red cup.
MID-LATE
   Ardour. Tall; gold and red.
   Dinkie. Greenish-yellow perianth, deep yellow cup with crinkled red edge.
   Russet. Dark red eye.

### IIIb. Small Cups. White Perianth, Cup Colored

There are many beautiful flowers in this section, some with very bright cups, some with just a delicate rim of color.

EARLY MIDSEASON

Angeline. Citron cup edged gold.
Pomona. Very white perianth, flat orange-red cup.

MIDSEASON

Cadence. Green cup, orange-red band at edge.
Kansas. Flat serrated crown rimmed apricot orange.
Lady Kesteven. Very white perianth, red eye.
Mahmoud. Bright red flat eye.
Matapan. Flat crimson eye.
Moina. Shallow crown edged salmon orange.
St. Louis. Flat yellow cup, red edge.

MID-LATE

Aircastle. Cup pale lemon edged deeper yellow.
Ballycastle. White cup edged orange-pink.
Bithynia. Flat cup edged apricot.
Blarney. Salmon cup edged yellow.
Clockface. Large; yellow crown.
Coloratura. Flaring cup edged with apricot frill.
Fairy Tale. Flat citron cup edged orange.
St. Anthony. Tall; small eye faintly tinged pink.
Sylvia O'Neill. Shallow frilled yellow cup.
Tebourba. Solid red cup.
Willowfield. Deep crimson cup.

LATE

Carnmoon. Eye with faint lemon rim.
*Corncrake. Large; orange-red eye.
Corofin. Flat yellow eye with broad crinkled bright red margin.
Dreamlight. Cup with narrow red rim.
Limerick. Dark red flat eye.
Lough Areema. Cup edged salmon.

* latest

Merlin. Flat yellow cup edged red.
\*Misty Moon. Soft pale salmon cup.
\*Reprieve. Pale cup frilled lemon.
\*Rockall. Bright red serrated cup.
Snow Gem. Tall; very white with red eye.

**IIIc. Small Cups. All White**

These beautiful flowers are neglected in nearly all general bulb lists. As they are late blooming, a little shade helps them to withstand heat waves which may force them open too quickly for their proper development.

MIDSEASON

Distingué. Long pointed tepals.
Moondance. Rather small flower with shallow crown.

MID-LATE

Chinese White. Large, circular perianth; shallow fluted crown.

LATE

Altyre. Tall, large; nearly flat eye.
Bryher. Tall; small eye touched green in center.
Polar Ice. Fluted eye, green in center.
Silver Salver. Flat eye.

VERY LATE

Alberni Beauty. Large, tall; flat palest yellow eye.
\*Cushendall. Flat frilled eye green in center. Stands heat.
\*Frigid. Flat fluted eye.
Polar Sea. Starry perianth; flat eye green in center.
Silvermine. Flat eye tinged green.
\*Silver Princess. Tiny creamy eye.

**IV. Doubles of Garden Origin** (one or more flowers to a stem)

There has been a great improvement in doubles. Many of the old varieties are coarse and blousy with a tendency to blast.

EARLY MIDSEASON

Golden Ducat. Full double, medium yellow.

\* latest

MIDSEASON
   Camellia. Neatly formed all yellow.
   Primrose Phoenix. An old variety of charm. Pale yellow.
   Snowball. White. Regular perianth; double center. Fragrant.
   Swansdown. Regular perianth; feathery double center. All white.
   White Lion. White with pale yellow center segments.
LATE
   Cheerfulness. Three to five flowers to a stem, cream and pale yellow.
   Double Event. White segments interspersed with pale yellow in center.
   Mary Copeland. White with short orange segments interspersed in center.
   Yellow Cheerfulness. Uniform yellow counterpart of 'Cheerfulness.'
VERY LATE
   Falaise. Fragrant white; orange-red segments interspersed through center.
   Rose of May. All white; fragrant.
   For doubles that are wild, or reputedly so, see Division X.

**V. Triandrus of Garden Origin**
   One to several flowers to a scape (usually two or three), drooping a little, sometimes a little reflexed. White or pale yellow or both; a few with some pink or red in the cup. Range from about 10 to 20 inches tall.

**Va. Long Cups**
EARLY MIDSEASON
   Lemon Drops. 16 inches. Soft yellow.
   Yellow Warbler. 14 inches. Pale soft yellow.
MIDSEASON
   Cathedral. 14 inches. White; broad bell-shaped cup.
   Forty-niner. 12 inches. Light yellow. Long season of bloom.
   Moonshine. 18 inches. White.
   Shot Silk. 18 inches. Creamy white.

Stoke. 12 inches. Pale yellow.

Tresamble. 18 inches. White; sometimes four or five flowers to a scape.

### Vb. Short Cups
EARLY MIDSEASON

Ivory Gate. 12 inches. Ivory white.

MIDSEASON

Rosedown. 15 inches. Bright yellow; goblet-shaped soft red-orange cup.

MID-LATE

Cobweb. 12 inches. White; pale yellow cup.

Oconee. 16 inches. White; pale yellow flat cup.

LATE

Sidhe. 14 inches. Pale yellow; flat cup.

Thoughtful. 12 inches. Softest yellow.

VERY LATE

Silver Chimes. 18 inches. Five to ten creamy fragrant flowers to a scape, a little tender. All stock may have virus; watch for yellow stripe.

### VI. Cyclamineus Varieties of Garden Origin

Usually one flower to a stem, long trumpet, tepals much reflexed, early, bright yellow. Exceptions to all these traits. About 8 to 18 inches high.

### VIa. Long Cups
EARLY

*Cornet. 10 inches. Bright yellow.

Dove Wings. 14 inches. White with soft yellow cup.

February Gold. 14 inches. Bright yellow, very vigorous.

February Silver. 14 inches. Creamy, cup a little deeper cream.

*Jana. 8 inches. Like 'Cornet,' but earlier. Late March in Philadelphia area.

March Breeze. 12 inches. Yellow, cup deeper.

* earliest

EARLY MIDSEASON
>Baby Doll (Caerhays). 10 inches. Small, with long trumpet. Yellow.
>>Charity May. 14 inches. Soft yellow; lovely form.
>>Chickadee. 10 inches. Soft yellow; orange cup.

MIDSEASON
>>Jenny. 15 inches. Short, creamy cup.
>>Larkelly. 12 inches. Yellow; orange cup.

**VIb. Short Cups**

MIDSEASON
>>Beryl. 10 inches. Soft yellow; deeper cup.
>>Roger. 10 inches. Yellow; orange-red cup.

**VII. Jonquil Varieties of Garden Origin**

>Usually more than one flower to a scape, fragrant, yellow, short-cupped; but exceptions to all these traits. Leaves of many are rather round in cross section. Range from 8 to 24 inches high.

**VIIa. Long Cups**

EARLY
>>Shah. 20 inches. Fragrant. One smooth bright yellow flower to a scape.

MIDSEASON
>>Fairy Nymph. 12 inches. Pale bicolor.
>>Golden Sceptre. 15 inches. Yellow.
>>Sweetness. 12 inches. Yellow.
>>White Wedgwood. 14 inches. Creamy.

**VIIb. Short Cups**

MIDSEASON
>>Golden Perfection. 24 inches. Large gold.
>>Orange Queen. 15 inches. All deep orange.
>>Sugarbush. 15 inches. White; pale yellow cup.
>>Trevithian. 20 inches. Soft yellow.

MID-LATE
>>Chérie. 18 inches. Ivory; pale pink cup.

Cheyenne. 18 inches. Cream and ivory.
Cora Ann. 14 inches. White; pale yellow cup.
Kiowa. 17 inches. Creamy.
LATE
Nirvana. 15 inches. White; fragrant.
*Tittle-Tattle. 18 inches. Yellow; shallow golden cup.
### VIII. Tazetta Varieties of Garden Origin

Tazetta varieties undiluted by other species are too tender for Northern gardens. Hybrids with the poet's narcissus have produced the race known as *poetaz,* varieties of which are hardier, but still not for the coldest gardens. They bear small-cupped flowers, fragrant, from two or three to about eight on a scape. They range from 14 to 24 inches in height. The following are poetaz varieties:

EARLY MIDSEASON
Cragford. Short. White; red cup.
Early Splendour. White; deep orange cup.
MIDSEASON
Laurens Koster. Tall. White, orange cup.
Matador. Yellow, orange-red cup.
Orange Wonder. White, orange-red cup.
Scarlet Gem. Yellow, bright orange-red cup.
MID-LATE
Martha Washington. Tall. White; yellow cup edged red. Two or three flowers to a scape.
LATE
Geranium. White; orange-red cup.

The pure tazettas (polyanthus narcissus) can be grown in milder areas: on the Eastern Shore of Maryland and Virginia, and from other mild sections southward. Since their foliage comes up in the fall, or in winter mild spells, they should have protection from freezing winds. Or success may result where

* latest

they are on the borderline of their hardiness by planting them on northern slopes which cool off more quickly in fall, and are less affected by winter warm spells, and mulching, to retard early growth. Tazettas like ample moisture. They are very fragrant, and have as many as twelve to twenty flowers in a cluster. The flowers are smaller than those of the poetaz. The "Paper White" is the best known of the tazetta varieties. Among others are 'Grand Emperor' (white; orange cup), 'Grande Monarque' (white; citron cup), 'Grand Primo Citronière' (white; citron cup), 'Grand Soleil d'Or' (yellow; orange cup), 'Scilly White' (white; creamy cup). Most are hard to obtain. Bulbs under local names are to be found in the Southern states, and are worth trying.

### IX. Poets of Garden Origin

The poets have one flower to a scape. The perianth is white, the small eye is red, orange, or yellow, usually deeper at the rim. They are late blooming. Heights range from about 15 to 20 inches.

MIDSEASON

Actaea. Tall. The largest poet. Red-edged eye.

MID-LATE

Shanach. Pale yellow eye, red rim.

Smyrna. Flat orange-red eye.

LATE

Cantabile. Small flower; green eye edged red.

*Dactyl. Flat citron eye edged red.

*Lamplighter. Solid red eye.

*Lights Out. Solid red eye.

Milan. Large; pale yellow eye, green center, red rim.

Sea-green. Pale green eye edged red.

### X. Species and Wild Forms and Hybrids

DOUBLES THAT ARE WILD OR REPUTEDLY SO

*Narcissus poeticus flore pleno* (*Albus Plenus Odoratus*). The

\* latest

fragrant double poet, very late, which is usually a very poor bloomer. Try 'Falaise' or 'Rose of May' in its place.

*N. telemonius plenus,* van Sion. The persistent old greenish-yellow found in old gardens. If bulbs are divided and reset, they are apt to show marked improvement in color and form. Very early.

WILD SPECIES AND VARIETIES OF THE JONQUIL SECTION

Some nine or ten species and their varieties have characteristics in common which make it logical to group them together botanically as the Jonquil Section of the genus *Narcissus.* The word *jonquil* is connected with the Latin word *juncus,* a rush, and refers to the rush-like foliage of several of the species, typified by *Narcissus jonquilla.* The foliage is dark green, and rounded in cross section. Members of the rush-leaved group have flowers that are yellow, fragrant, and borne several to a scape. The other species in the section have flowers white or yellow, one or several to a scape, and have glaucous (grayish) leaves. Those of the latter group are plants for the careful specialist, as they are small and not easy to grow. One of them, *N. watieri,* with single starry white flowers on 4-inch scapes is now seen in flower shows. There are also a number of wild hybrids of great vigor which have obvious jonquil characteristics.

This rather lengthy explanation will perhaps be helpful to those who call all yellow daffodils jonquils.

*Narcissus jonquilla,* Jonquil. South Europe and Algeria. 12 inches. Small, smooth, yellow, very fragrant, with two to six small flowers with very small cups to a scape, in midseason. Rush-like leaves. It grows very well in the Philadelphia area and to the south, but farther north is not satisfactory. It is often listed as *N. jonquilla simplex* in catalogs, while bulbs bought as *N. jonquilla* are apt to turn out to be the campernelle.

*N. odorus,* Campernelle. Wild hybrid of the jonquil with a trumpet daffodil. The leaves are a little wider, the cup longer than that of the jonquil, the flower larger. Widespread, perhaps in more than one form, in the Southern states, escaping from old gardens.

*N. odorus rugulosus.* A variety of the campernelle, a little shorter, but the flowers somewhat larger.

*N. tenuior.* 10 inches. Late-flowering pale yellow hybrid with the poet's narcissus.

WILD VARIETIES AND FORMS OF *Narcissus Poeticus*

*Narcissus ornatus.* A form of *exertus,* a variety of the subspecies *radiiflorus.* 13 inches. Midseason. Broad eye rimmed scarlet.

*N. poeticus radiiflorus.* Small flowers, very starry, in late midseason.

*N. poeticus recurvus,* Pheasant's Eye. Very late small fragrant flowers, cup edged deep red, perianth reflexed.

**XI. Miscellaneous Narcissi**

Those that have no place in the other divisions at present consist of two groups: small garden hybrids of *N. bulbocodium* (hoop-petticoat daffodil) and standard-size freakish garden flowers the structure of which excludes them from other divisions. The coronas of the following two varieties, for example, are so slashed into segments that they cannot be called trumpets, crowns, or cups.

Hillbilly. 18 inches. Midseason. Light yellow crown divided into six segments which lie back against the perianth.

Split. Perianth white, crown divided into many pale yellow segments.

## DAFFODILS IN THE GARDEN PICTURE

In our area, we can count on about six weeks of bloom from daffodils, but sometimes it stretches to eight, skimpy, of course, at both ends. It begins the last part of March, and extends toward the middle of May. Places for daffodils can usually be found where they will be a dominant part of the spring picture, but where later bloom in other parts of the grounds will be em-

88  *Hardy Garden Bulbs*

phatic enough to attract full attention when they have gone by. The long period of six to eight weeks required for the ripening of the copious foliage must be considered.

In mixed flower beds, it is best to place them far enough

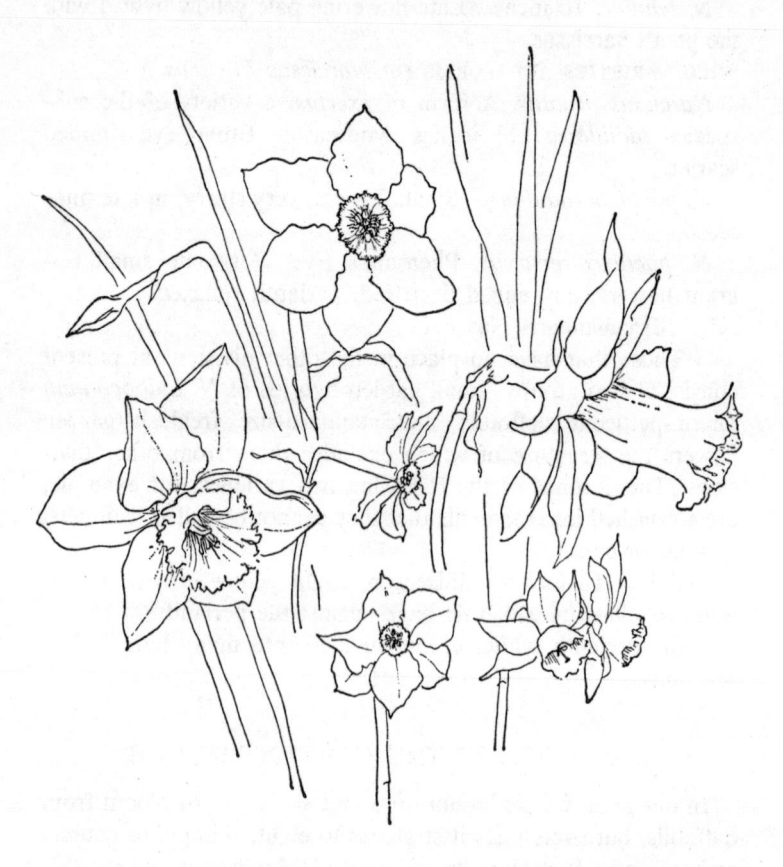

Daffodil forms. Clockwise, left to right, a large cup (Division II), a small cup (Division III), a trumpet (Division I), a triandrus hybrid (Division V), and a garden poet (Division IX). In the center is a wild poet (Division X).

back from the front edge so that later-flowering plants may grow up to a height that will more or less conceal them when their bloom is finished. The young foliage of many perennials makes a good setting for them.

They can be planted in front of shrub borders, but should be kept far enough away from masses of roots and closely overhanging branches for healthy growth. They are wonderful for naturalizing in thin woodlands and for planting in masses where there is spring sun but too much summer shade for the usual perennials.

They can also be planted in grass that is kept in a rather meadow-like condition with infrequent mowing. If the grass is cut, as usually it must be, before the daffodil foliage has ripened, care must be taken to avoid the daffodil clumps.

Daffodils do well in ground covers such as pachysandra, ivy, and periwinkle if there has been good soil preparation and if they are under deep-rooting trees like oaks. Low-branched trees like beeches and lindens which have masses of surface roots do not give bulbs much chance.

Nevertheless, on the small place where there is a much-needed shade tree, it is surprising what can be done with daffodils when even a blade of grass cannot be grown under the tree —if you work up the ground as thoroughly as possible, using larger quantities than usual of peat moss, leaf mold, compost, or other forms of humus. Perhaps a lower limb or two of the tree can be removed. If much soil has eroded from over the tree roots, add a cubic yard or two of good topsoil. You may need to put in an edging of rocks or long logs to keep it from washing away again.

Plant vigorous and inexpensive daffodils such as 'Fortune' and 'Carlton,' some scillas, both early and late kinds, some low ferns, and English ivy. Give the ground an extra good soaking from time to time—as needed in the spring, and every two or three weeks in summer. Once a year give a good top dressing of organic material and a scattering of fertilizer. You won't have prize flowers, but you will have a pleasant spot instead of a barren one. You should also have a healthier tree.

The choicest daffodils should, of course, have the choicest spots. If they are planted in a mixed border, special care should be taken to be sure they are not crowded. Even single bulbs can be planted, alternated with groups of three or more to avoid a spotty effect. The gardener who begins growing daffodils as a hobby soon finds himself buying single bulbs, or three of a kind, rather than ten or a dozen. He knows his single bulb will increase, and that the second or third year after its first bloom he can dig it and spread out the increase to make a little group. Perhaps he will then trade a bulb with a fellow fancier.

In the perennial border three to a dozen bulbs in a clump are enough. While a tulip bulb gives but a single flower, new double-nosed daffodil bulbs are apt to give two at least, and the second year are likely to give more.

In plantings featuring daffodils by themselves, larger numbers of each kind are needed. In a small birch grove, for example, groups might vary from fifty to several hundred of a kind. The tasseled catkins of birches are especially charming with daffodils. The medium- and small-cupped varieties seem better suited to semi-wild plantings than the large trumpets.

In places with considerable summer shade, ferns are very useful to give greenery when the daffodil foliage has gone. Christmas fern, New York fern, evergreen wood fern, cinnamon and interrupted ferns are especially good. Avoid the coarse, fast-spreading bracken.

We have daffodils and hay-scented fern planted together in the sun, but I think the fern, which forms extensive mats of creeping rootstocks, is a little overwhelming, although we thin it from time to time. However, the delicate young fronds do look charming with the daffodils that are vigorous growers and can compete with them.

COMPANIONS FOR DAFFODILS. Pale and white daffodils go

with any other flowers; the strong yellow and red-cupped kinds are best kept apart from pinks and crimsons. White magnolias, crab apples, and flowering cherries, pale yellow corylopsis, other spring bulbs and early perennials in blues and lavenders act as peacemakers so that deep pink cherries and crab apples, crimson magnolias and rosy purple rhododendrons can be brought into the picture.

Rhododendrons and mountain laurel make splendid foils for daffodils, and can be planned for later bloom to brighten the same scene when the early flowers are gone. Japanese hollies, yews, leucothoë, and other evergreens make good background material. Yews will stand the cold where broadleafed evergreens will not. The sturdy deciduous shrubs of colder climates can have foreground plantings of daffodils.

PRICE CONSIDERATIONS. Those who venture for the first time into the wider fields of daffodil culture may be shocked by the prices of novelties, unless they have been conditioned by forays into other plant specialties such as iris. They may find it incredible that fine new varieties may be priced as high as $75 for one bulb. When the famous daffodil 'Fortune' was introduced in 1923, bulbs were $125 each! Now they can be had for twenty cents, but the variety is still held in high regard. Few can buy high-priced varieties, but part of the fun is watching each year to see if the coveted ones have come within reach.

SIZE ISN'T EVERYTHING. A group of tall, stately 'St. Egwin,' the great snowy flowers of 'Vigil,' are a splendid sight. But the varieties that are shorter and smaller not only set them off, making them look larger and taller by comparison, but have a very special charm of their own. 'Nakota,' 'Dove Wings,' and 'Ivory Gate,' 'Cornet,' and 'March Breeze,' a host of others, can claim small size as an asset.

In many situations the scale of the smaller flowers is more suitable and more satisfying. They have a definite contribution to make to small places as well as adding variety to any planting.

## SMALL DAFFODILS

There is no definite line to be drawn between large and small daffodils. In all the divisions there is variation in height and flower size. However, the really small ones need and deserve a setting all their own. They need locations where they can be seen to advantage, and where they will not be swallowed up amid larger plants, or damaged during gardening operations. They are perfect, of course, for rock gardens. We grow our own on the top of a dry retaining wall which is high enough so that we can look easily into the little faces, and where we can also grow other small plants which combine well with them.

For the most part, the daffodil species of small stature are difficult to grow. It is unfortunate that they, rather than small garden varieties, are offered in most catalogs as miniatures. They are all too apt to have been collected from the wild, thereby threatening the survival of some in a wild state. *Narcissus cyclamineus* is one that is in danger of extinction in its native land. Some dealers offer the species grown from seed, and these are better bulbs to buy, but also a little higher in price. They are specified as home-grown in the catalogs.

Other plants listed as miniatures often turn out to be not so very small. 'February Gold,' for example, and 'Thalia' are far too large for that designation.

Unlike the small species, most of the small garden varieties are not hard to grow. To have them is to love them, and to want more. Then comes the frustration of finding that the supply is limited and the listings are meager. However, with interest in them increasing, and several breeders working to produce new varieties, the future holds promise.

Garden varieties of small daffodils do not differ from the larger ones in their cultural requirements. However, in order to keep them from growing too luxuriantly and losing some of their valued small size, they should be kept on a rather thin diet. Nitrogen especially should be avoided. A heavy soil should be lightened with some coarse sand and peat moss.

The ones listed here, while all small, may not all be considered as miniatures. However, they are of a scale which makes them suitable for use with small rather than large plants.

### I. Trumpets of Garden Origin

Bambi. Bicolor. 6 inches. Very early, free-flowering, increases well.

Little Beauty. Bicolor. 5 inches. Very early. Good proportions.

Rockery Gem. White. 10 inches. Opens cream, fades white.

Sneezy. All yellow. 5 inches. Early.

Tanagra. All yellow. 6 inches. Very early. Excellent form and proportion.

W. P. Milner. Ivory white. 10 inches. Early. Flowers droop a little.

Wee Bee. Light yellow. 5 inches. Early.

### II. Large Cups of Garden Origin

(The word "large" here is a matter of proportion to the perianth)

Goldsithney. All yellow. 9 inches. Free-flowering; early midseason.

Lady Bee. White, pink cup. 10 inches. Early midseason.

Nor-Nor. Perianth yellow turning white; cup yellow turning orange. 10 inches. Early midseason.

### III. Small Cups of Garden Origin

Xit. Pure white. 7 inches. Mid-late.

### IV. Doubles of Garden Origin

Kehelland. Double yellow trumpet. 7 inches. Midseason.

Pencrebar (Queen Anne's Double Jonquil). One or two yellow flowers to a scape. 7 inches. Mid-late.

Both these are very apt to blast (flower buds fail to develop). Give partial shade and a moist spot.

### V. Triandrus of Garden Origin

April Tears. Yellow; cup paler than perianth. 6 inches. Two to six flowers to a scape.

Arctic Morn. White; pink tinge to cup. 8 inches. Two to four flowers to scape.

Kenellis. Creamy. 6 inches. Tepals small in proportion to widely flaring cup. Cross with a bulbocodium (hoop petticoat).

Samba. Yellow; red of cup suffusing perianth. 9 inches. Midseason.

### VI. Cyclamineus of Garden Origin

Greenshank. Pale yellow. 6 inches. Long trumpet points to the ground; perianth swept straight back. Early midseason.

Jumblie. Yellow. 8 inches. Early.

Tête-à-Tête. Two yellow flowers to a scape. 6 inches. Early.

### VII. Jonquils of Garden Origin

Bobbysoxer. Yellow. 7 inches. Two to three very neat flowers to a scape, small cups deeper than perianth. Mid-late.

Flomay. White; cup edged buff pink. 6 inches. One flower to scape. Midseason.

Kidling. Several small all-yellow fragrant flowers to a scape. 6 inches high when it begins its long blooming season, reaching 10 inches. Profuse bloom, increases well. Seems to be hardier than *N. jonquilla,* which it resembles.

Lintie. Yellow; orange-red cup. 10 inches. One to three flowers to scape. Mid-late.

Sundial. Yellow; deeper-colored small cup; very neat. Two to three flowers to scape. Early midseason.

### VIII. Tazettas of Garden Origin (not for cold areas)

Cyclataz. Yellow; orange cup. 7 inches. Three to four flowers to scape. Early.

Halingy. White and cream. 7 inches. Early; several flowers to scape.

### X. Species and Wild Varieties and Hybrids

*N. asturiensis* (*N. minimus*). This tiny golden trumpet is one worth trying. It is quite hardy. 4 inches. Very early. Cover with two inches of soil.

*N. bulbocodium,* Hoop-Petticoat Daffodil. The name well describes the appearance of the flower, with very small pointed tepals and wide-flaring corona. Forms vary from bright yellow to white. The yellow *N. b. conspicuus* (6 inches) is early and dependable. Cover with two inches of soil. It blooms in three years from seed, and is a good one to try this way. *N. bulbocodium* foliage makes its growth in the fall. The fine grassy foliage withstands freezing well, but is better if protected from winter winds.

PLANTING DEPTHS. Small bulbs may be covered with only two inches of soil. They are, therefore, more subject to drying out, which will hasten browning of the foliage. Extra leaf mold or peat moss and some extra water during spring droughts will help them. Bulbs of the garden varieties of miniatures vary in size, and the larger ones can be covered four inches.

COMPANIONS FOR SMALL DAFFODILS. Thymes, the smaller sedums, and other very low plants are in scale with the littlest ones. They may be allowed to creep over the bulbs in summer, and carefully thinned as necessary. Even the wild pussytoes (*Antennaria* species), lawn weeds with rosettes of gray leaves, can be used with them. Of course there are many choicer rock plants, often more difficult to procure, which are fine companions.

The tiny pansy faces of johnny-jump-ups are perfect, and the plants seed themselves freely. As spring goes on, they must sometimes be cut back, or pushed aside from the daffodils. White arabis and white or lavender creeping phlox (*Phlox subulata*) are easy to get, but too large and thick to be close to the tiniest, though they may be used if kept a little apart.

In summer, small annuals may be sown over the bulbs. Sweet alyssum, portulaca, and the smallest varieties of marigolds and zinnias are easy, and suitable in some locations, but not in rock gardens. For these, the small fine-leaved golden Dahlberg daisy (*Thymophylla tenuiloba*) is better. It is not always easy to find seed, but it is listed in some catalogs.

# CHAPTER VI

# Tulips

Everyone loves the tall tulips of late spring, stately in regal purple and crimson or gay in scarlet, pink, or yellow. Never were flowers more entitled to the overworked adjective "gorgeous." What a loss it would be to our gardens if we had to do without those wonderful globes of color!

Yet before these best-known varieties reach their peak, there are tulips of many sizes and colors ready to make early spring gardens brighter if they are only given a chance. It seems strange that such gay and hardy flowers are not better known and more used.

There are some 150 species of *Tulipa,* a genus of the Lily Family. They grow from the mild regions around the Mediterranean, across southern Russia, Turkey, and Persia, up into Turkestan, Siberia, down into Kashmir, and on to China. In lands now closed to Western plant explorers there must be many species not yet collected for garden trials.

They range from tiny, starry flowers only a few inches high to flowers four inches long on stems 18 or 20 inches high. In color, they go from pale lavender and soft pink and cream to bright yellows, scarlets, orange, cherry, and combinations of these. In shape, the flowers may be oval, quite rounded, long and pointed, urn-shaped or egg-shaped. Usually the flowers

This fine collection of daffodils in the garden of two connoisseurs will be followed by choice collections of bearded iris and daylilies, many of their own breeding.

*Narcissus gracilis* is a wild hybrid between *Narcissus jonquilla* and *Narcissus poeticus*.

*Above.* Daffodil 'Corofin' is the result of hybridization and selection by a skilled plant breeder.

*Below.* The beauty of Dutch hyacinths is enhanced by pansies and English daisies.

*Above.* May-flowering tulips with arabis, hardy candytuft, and pansies.
*Upper right.* Tulips after digging, showing how each bulb divided. Large bulbs will bloom the next year; smaller ones need two or more years to reach flowering size.
*Lower right.* Tulip bulbs after cleaning, sorting, and counting, packed in old nylon stockings for summer storage. They will be hung in a cool, airy garage.

*Above.* Hybrids of *Tulipa fosteriana,* in variations of cherry rose, pale yellow, and cream, bloom gaily while the tall late tulips at upper left are still in tight bud.

*Below. Tulipa turkestanica* has clusters of small starry flowers of white and cream on 8-inch stems.

are upright, but a few are prone to face sideways. According to species, they produce one, two, or several flowers to a stem.

The older garden tulips are considered to be derived from two species. The common tulip, parent of the tall late varieties, is called *Tulipa gesneriana,* supposedly of Asia Minor and Persia. But these tall beauties of our late spring gardens are ladies of mysterious background. So long have they been cultivated that their beginnings are not known. It was as long-cherished garden flowers that they were brought to Western Europe from Turkey, supposedly about 1554, but they may have been known in some parts of Europe much earlier. Everyone knows that in Holland the tulip became an object of such esteem that it was the cause of that phenomenon known as the tulipomania, when extraordinary prices were paid for bulbs. The bubble burst, but after a period of inactivity, Holland developed the sound and important bulb industry that exists today.

The earlier and shorter garden tulips are assigned to the species *T. suaveolens,* supposedly native from southern Russia to Persia, but that, too, is only guessing. However, the value of these bright-hued flowers is not guesswork.

In addition to about 3,000 garden varieties descended from these ancient garden flowers, modern hybridists are busy creating new classes of garden hybrids, using other tulip species. In fact, Degenaar de Jager remarks in *The Daffodil and Tulip Yearbook 1961* of the Royal Horticultural Society that "The rage for new varieties by the Dutch growers seems to be utterly extravagant nowadays, and has taken the form of a mania." The handsome results of this mania can be seen in the displays of new varieties in the famous Keukenhof Gardens in the Netherlands and in the gardens at Sterling Forest about thirty miles north of New York City. Many of them have found their way to bulb dealers in this country, and while the rarest novelties are often higher in price, already many of these new tulips cost no more than the ones that have been in commerce for years.

## CULTURE

Garden tulips are usually not long lived. The first year they give good flowers of uniform size and height. For the second and third years they should be effective, but after that they are apt to be spotty. However, they are not very expensive. The average garden can be planned so that a third of the tulips can be replaced each year. Those which are removed for replacement may yield some bulbs large enough to go into the cutting garden, or to be replanted in smaller groups.

Tulip planting is one of the late gardening jobs of the year, but early ordering or buying ensures getting the kinds wanted. The bulbs should be kept cool and open to the air, but away from frost, until planting time, which should be before the ground freezes. If you are caught by cold, a mattock will lift the frozen layer of ground and the bulbs can be planted in the soft earth underneath. The deeper the frost the greater the difficulty, but the bulbs should not be held any longer than necessary once the planting season has arrived.

The Dutch Bulb Growers Association recommends planting tulips six to eight inches deep except in heavy clays, where four to five inches is sufficient. The deeper planting makes it easier to cultivate and to grow annuals over the bulbs during the summer without injuring them, but makes it harder to get them out when the time comes to lift them. Shallower planting is called for if they are to be dug every year. Place the bulbs five or six inches apart.

WINTER AND SPRING CARE. Mulching for winter protection depends on climate: in severe climates, it is necessary. Wait until the ground is frozen before putting on the mulch so that it will not become a cover for burrowing mice or a haven for slugs and insects. But where freezing can go deep, put it on when the top two or three inches of soil are frozen. Two to four inches of straw with a rough topping of corn stalks or branches that will catch and hold snow may be needed. In our moderate area, we do not put a winter mulch on tulips.

Heavy mulches should be removed a little at a time, in two or three stages, as soon as the plants start to come through the ground in spring, preferably on still, cloudy days, to accustom the young growth by degrees to sun and wind.

After the new shoots are well up, light surface cultivation to break up the ground will check weed growth at the beginning and admit water. A little fertilizer, such as a 5-10-10 or the same fertilizer used for daffodils, can be sprinkled among the plants and scratched in, but in average soils this is just for extra size and quality. The flowers will do very well without it. We often get hot, dry spells for a few days in spring, and then a good watering is called for. Water early in the day so the plants will dry off before night, and soak the soil, avoiding the foliage if possible. Heavy sprinkling when the flower stems have just shot up and are soft may put bends in them which will not fully straighten.

HANDLING REPLACEMENTS. When tulips are dug with replanting of the same bulbs in mind, the foliage must be allowed to complete its important function of making food to be stored in the bulb for the next spring. The bulbs should either be left in place until the foliage starts to turn yellow, or dug and heeled-in in another location where the leaves can continue their work. Either way, digging must be careful to avoid injury to the bulbs.

If they are to be heeled-in elsewhere, digging must be even more careful, to keep from breaking the stem and those precious leaves. (For the process of heeling-in, *see* Glossary.) When the tops have turned yellow and dry, lift the bulbs carefully and remove the old stems and leaves. There will be bulbs of different sizes covered with new bright brown coats enclosed, one or more together, in the old coats, now dull and disintegrating. Remove the old coats.

Allow the bulbs to dry for a day or so in a cool shady place, whether they have been dug direct from the garden or from the heeling-in trench. A garage floor is often a good place. Then store in flats, onion bags, or other well-ventilated containers.

Always handle bulbs carefully to avoid bruises and cuts where disease organisms can start. Discard any that are damaged or look unhealthy.

Be sure that labels are kept with each separate batch of bulbs, unless they are to be planted in a cutting garden where identification does not matter.

REPLANTING. When autumn rolls around, sort over the bulbs, and discard those that are in poor condition or very small. Varieties differ in the way they divide and multiply. Some will give a reasonable number of bulbs that are large enough to bloom the next year. Others give many small bulbs and few good-sized ones. New ones of the same kinds may be added to bring each variety up to the number wanted, or they may be planted in smaller groups, or transferred to other parts of the grounds.

REPLANTING VERSUS NEW BULBS. One reason for digging tulip bulbs is to give them a dry summer. Most tulip ancestors are inhabitants of lands cold in winter and hot and dry in summer. If kept in flower beds, they get either rain or artificial watering during the season when they should be dry. The gardener who has the time and strength to dig, store, and replant can keep his tulips going a long time without replacements. By growing the smaller bulbs to blooming size he can increase his stock.

But where summer storage room is poor and time scarce, or paid labor involved, it is probably cheaper to buy new bulbs when the bloom of a group lessens. Then dig them out for discard as soon as they have finished flowering, and replace them in the fall with new bulbs.

ROTATION. Many garden plants can be rotated to their advantage, and many need dividing every year or so to keep them vigorous and in good blooming condition. Tulips should be part of any rotation scheme that can be worked out. If a clump is discarded at the end of several years, plant iris or some other frequently divided plant in its place, and plant the new clump of tulips where the iris has been.

## DISEASES

As the tulips grow, watch for signs of botrytis or tulip fire. It is a fungus disease that is worse in wet weather and in areas where poor air circulation and morning shade keep plants covered with moisture for long periods.

A reddish instead of green color and patches of mold are danger signals. Deformed leaves and flower buds that are dark and shrunken should be removed and dropped into a paper bag for burning. Remove the whole plant if it is seriously affected. Snap off faded flowers before the petals fall, because on the ground they may develop tulip fire, leaving spores to winter over and infect plants the next spring. Dispose of these by way of a paper bag, too.

Where botrytis is a problem, the tulips may be sprayed with Fermate, first when growth is a few inches high, and later to cover the foliage when it is well grown. Inspection and sanitation should be continued until the ripened stalk and foliage can be cut to the ground and burned. Bulbs can carry over the infection. Discard any that have sunken discolored areas.

Another significant disease is the virus that results in *breaking,* or striping and feathering of the flower color. Any tulips that are supposed to be solid colors which show striping should be removed and burned. The virus which causes the striping can be spread by aphids. "Broken" tulips are discussed later in this chapter.

Moles can be a serious pest of tulips. We are told that they do not eat the bulbs, but they certainly bite through any stems that happen to be in the way of tunneling operations. Mice use the tunnels to reach the bulbs conveniently. Chipmunks, squirrels, and rabbits also are tulip pests.

## CLASSES AND VARIETIES OF TULIPS

The garden varieties of tulips are invaluable for their wide color range, from pure white through pale yellow, pink, and lilac, to deeper shades, reds, oranges, golds, deep rose, purple-violets, and blends and muted tones of all these. There are no blues. The so-called blues, violet-blues, or lavender-blues all actually contain a good deal of red. The red is more dominant when the flowers first open, an important point to remember when planning color schemes. As these flowers mature, the red slowly fades, leaving silvery lilacs, violets, and purples. The bluest blue in tulips is to be found in the bases of many varieties and some of the species.

Making lists of varieties is a diverting occupation, but it is easy to question their usefulness. The most that any list-maker can hope to do is to indicate the range to be found in each class. Many standard varieties appear in most catalogs. Many other rarer but delightful varieties appear in one catalog or another, but are not generally available. Even though you cling to your favorite varieties, try some new ones, too, when you make replacements. Send for catalogs you haven't had before. Above all, don't stick to the tall May tulips. Try some of the earlier kinds. Be brave! Live it up! You have delightful surprises ahead.

Tulips have been classified into twenty-three divisions by a joint committee of the Royal Horticultural Society and the Royal General Dutch Bulb Growers Society. They are listed here. There are a number of other classifications sometimes used in catalogs, but they are not officially recognized and tend to cause confusion.

**Division 1. Duc van Tol Tulips**

Of historical importance only. Low-growing, very early, bright colors. Superseded by Single Early Tulips.

**Division 2. Single Early Tulips**

In the Philadelphia area, these bloom about mid-April. They are low, varying from about 10 to 16 inches in height. They are often confused with the later and taller Cottage Tulips.

When varieties are designated E (early), M (midseason), or L (late), this refers to comparative blooming time for the division.

WHITE

Diana. E 14 inches.

White Hawk. M 13 inches.

YELLOW

Apricot Yellow. M 14 inches, buff-yellow tinged soft orange.

Bellona. M 16 inches, golden yellow.

Mme. Gevers. M 14 inches, pale.

Rising Sun. M 14 inches, bright yellow.

ORANGE

Fred Moore. E 15 inches, soft brownish orange.

General de Wet. M 15 inches, bright orange and gold blend. Fragrant.

Prince of Austria. M 15 inches, bright scarlet suffused orange.

Princess Irene. Terra cotta suffused purple.

Sunburst. M 12 inches, golden yellow flushed red.

PINK

Diadem. L 14 inches, soft rose.

Ibis. M 14 inches, deep rose, lighter edge.

Pink Beauty. L 14 inches, deep rose-pink, white stripe on outer tepals.

RED

Bel Ami. Rose-red edged silver.

Couleur Cardinal. L 14 inches, crimson-red, dusted gray outside.

PURPLE

Van der Neer. M 13 inches, soft violet-purple.

RED AND YELLOW

Keizerskroon. M 15 inches. Bright scarlet, broad edge of bright golden-yellow. Not easy to blend into a mixed planting.

Prince Carnaval. M 15 inches. Golden yellow, center of each tepal flamed with scarlet. More interesting and less harsh than Keizerskroon.

### Division 3. Double Early Tulips

In the Philadelphia area, blooming about mid-April. Stems stout, flowers large, opening into full rosettes often 4 inches across. 10 to 14 inches in height.

WHITE

Murillo. M 12 inches. White with pink flush.
Schnoonoord. M 11 inches.

YELLOW

Hoangho. M 14 inches. Pure yellow.
Maréchal Niel. M 12 inches. Pale yellow touched orange, turning orange.
Mr. van der Hoef. M 12 inches. Bright yellow.
Tea-Rose. M 12 inches. Soft yellow flushed salmon, turning salmon-rose.

ORANGE

Orange Nassau. M 12 inches. Orange-red.

PINK TO ROSE

Electra. M 12 inches. Violet-rose.
Peach Blossom. M 12 inches. Deep rose.

RED

Scarlet Cardinal. E 10 inches. Bright scarlet.
Vuurbaak. E 10 inches. Scarlet.
Willemsoord. M 12 inches. Carmine edged white.

The early tulips, very gay, are good for a show of color where they can be seen easily from house or entrance walk. Their low stature makes them adaptable for formal massing and for use in front of low foundation plantings. They are not suitable for rock gardens, where the species tulips offer better choices. In large mixed borders, the space is better devoted to later tulips, when there is more garden material to accompany them. However, there are often ways they can be used to make lovely little

pictures in conjunction with early-blooming trees and shrubs. Certainly they are not used as much as they should be.
**Division 4. Mendel Tulips**
A little later than Divisions 2 and 3. They are crosses between the Duc van Tols and the Darwins, and intermediate in height (about 14 to 20 inches). Used mostly for forcing.

Her Grace. 20 inches. Pure white, upper edges of tepals bright pink.
**Division 5. Triumph Tulips**
Crosses between Single Early and May-flowering tulips. Intermediate in size and time of bloom, a little later than the Mendels, and about 16 to 24 inches.
WHITE
Blizzard. 24 inches. Large creamy white.
Garden Party. 24 inches. White, edged bright rose.
Kansas. 16 inches. Pure white.
PINK
Airy. 20 inches. Pale lilac-rose.
Hadley. 23 inches. Light salmon-pink, flushed orange.
Kerbert (Mr. Kerbert). Bright rose-pink on white.
Northern Queen (Queen of the North). 20 inches. White edged bright pink.
RED
Alberio. 20 inches. Cherry-red edged yellow.
Aureola. 18 inches. Red edged gold.
Bandoeng. 20 inches. Mahogany-red flushed orange, lighter edge.
Crater. 18 inches. Bright red, passing into vermilion at edge.
Elmus. 18 inches. Cherry-red, white edge.
Korneforos. 24 inches. Crimson-red, brilliant.
PURPLE
Denbola. 20 inches. Deep purple-red edged cream.
Dreaming Maid. 18 inches. Violet edged white.
Modern Times. Purple-violet, edged lilac.

YELLOW
   Makassar. 20 inches. Deep yellow.
   Sulphur Glory. 22 inches. Pale.
ORANGE
   Johanna. 20 inches. Soft salmon-rose, white base.
   Nova. 22 inches. Blend of old rose, carmine and apricot.

**Division 7. Darwin Hybrid Tulips**

Listed here before Division 6 (Darwins) because of their earlier blooming time, result of the influence of *T. fosteriana,* the early-flowering bright scarlet species which is one of the parents. A fairly new class, most of the present ones variations of scarlet.

   Apeldoorn. 21 inches. Medium-size flowers, orange-scarlet, pale lilac sheen outside. Black base edged yellow.

   General Eisenhower. 26 inches. Large flowers, scarlet, with small black base edged yellow.

   Gudoshnik. 26 inches. Yellow stippled rose-red. This and several other yellows in this class may prove to be unstable, tending to revert to the reds from which they have sported.

   Oxford. 24 inches. Deep orange-scarlet, purple-red flush outside. Golden base.

**Divisions 6, 8, and 10. Darwin, Breeder, and Cottage Tulips**

I have combined these three divisions here because of the introduction of many new varieties that do not conform to the old distinctions that used to separate them from each other. They are all tall, and flower at the same time at the height of spring—mid-May in the Philadelphia area. Selection of varieties in these divisions for garden use can be made on the basis of color and height rather than division. The divisions are indicated by (D), (B), and (C) preceding each name.

WHITE TO CREAM
   (D) Annie Speelman. 28 inches. Cream.
   (D) Blanca. 22 inches. White with pale yellow anthers.
   (C) Carrara. 24 inches. Yellow anthers.

(D) Glacier. 28 inches. Ivory white, white anthers.
(C) Ivory Glory. 26 inches. Large, egg-shaped ivory.
(D) Mrs. Grullemans. 28 inches. Creamy white, yellow anthers.
(C) Mt. Erebus (correct name, White City). 28 inches. Pure white, yellow anthers.
(D) White Giant. 30 inches. Black anthers.
(D) Zwanenburg. 29 inches. All white; black anthers.

YELLOW

(C) Belle Jaune. 28 inches. Egg-shaped golden yellow.
(B) Cherbourg. Golden yellow, brushed purple.
(B) Garden Magic. 29 inches. Gold, faint brush of purple on outer tepals.
(D) Golden Age. 26 inches. Deep yellow, maturing orange at edges.
(C) Golden Harvest. 28 inches. Deep yellow.
(C) Mrs. John T. Scheepers. 30 inches. Long flower, medium light yellow.
(C) Mrs. Moon. 26 inches. Medium yellow, shape almost lily-flowered.
(D) Niphetos. 28 inches. Soft pale yellow, yellow anthers. Long-lasting.
(D) Sunkist. 30 inches. Bright golden yellow.
(B) Tantalus. 30 inches. Dull light yellow brushed lavender.
(D) Yellow Giant. 30 inches. Deep yellow, black anthers.

SOFT ORANGE TO SALMON AND SALMON-ROSE

(These can be used with pinks and rose-reds.)
(C) Artist. 20 inches. Soft green, rose, and salmon.
(C) Dido. 28 inches. Salmon-rose and amber.
(C) General de la Rey. 30 inches. Soft rose and apricot.
(C) Good Gracious. 28 inches. Soft amber, apricot, and pink.
(C) Marjorie Bowen. 30 inches. Salmon, buff, and rose.

ORANGE TO BRONZE

(Not at their best combined with pinks and rose-reds.)
(B) Dillenburg. 26 inches. Orange and gold, touch of rose.

(B) Don Eugo. 26 inches. Reddish brown.
(B) Indian Chief. 33 inches. Coppery red-brown.
(B) Orange Beauty (Prince of Orange). 24 inches. Bright orange, shaded bronze, edged yellow.
(B) Orange Delight. 28 inches. Bronze tinged orange.

BRONZE AND TERRA COTTA BLENDS

(B) Dixie Sunshine. 28 inches. Lavender, buff, and bronze.
(B) Panorama. 26 inches. Bronze and terra cotta.
(B) Penelope. 30 inches. Buff, bronze, and lavender.

LIGHT TO MEDIUM PINK

(D) Aristocrat. 28 inches. Soft violet rose.
(D) Clara Butt. 27 inches. Soft salmon-pink. Old favorite. Flower not large.
(D) Mr. van Zijl. 28 inches. Soft pure pink, paling to edges.
(D) Princess Elizabeth. 28 inches. Rose-pink, silvering to edges.
(D) Queen of the Bartigans. 27 inches. Clear pink, white base.
(D) Rosy O'Day. 28 inches. Very pale violet-rose.
(C) Rosy Wings. 29 inches. Salmon-rose.
(C) Smiling Queen. 30 inches. Bright pink, silvering to edges.
(D) The Peach. 26 inches. Rose-pink, cream base.

DEEPER PINK TO DEEP ROSE

(C) Chappaqua. 30 inches. Dark violet-rose.
(D) Elizabeth Arden. 28 inches. Dark salmon-rose.
(B) Katherine Truxton. Grayed rose, bronze edge.
(D) Margaux. 28 inches. Deep wine-rose.
(D) Notre Dame. 28 inches. Rose-red.
(D) Pride of Zwanenburg. 28 inches. Deep salmon-rose.

REDS

(D) Charles Needham. 25 inches. Bright red, dark blue base.
(D) City of Haarlem. 28 inches. Deep bright red, blue base.
(D) Eclipse. 29 inches. Deep bright red. Long lasting.
(D) Pride of Haarlem. 28 inches. Deep crimson-red. Combines well with pinks and roses.

ORANGE-RED TO RED

(Bright and beautiful, but often hard to combine with other tulips.)

(C) Advance. 30 inches. Bright salmon-red softened by dusky bloom. Early.

(B) Chinese Bandit. 28 inches. Chinese red overlaid orange-bronze.

(C) Marshal Haig. 30 inches. Scarlet-red.

(C) Mayflower. 30 inches. Crimson-scarlet.

(B) Moroccan Beauty. 28 inches. Bright red and mahogany-red, yellow base.

(B) Papago. 32 inches. Orange-red, yellow base.

LILAC TO PURPLE AND VIOLET

(D) Archbishop. 28 inches. Deep lilac-purple.

(B) Bacchus. 30 inches. Deep violet-purple.

(D) Bleu Aimable. 26 inches. Lilac.

(D) Cum Laude. 29 inches. Violet.

(D) Demeter. 30 inches. Purple. Early, long lasting.

(D) Denver. 30 inches. Blue-violet.

(D) Djingez Chan. 30 inches. Purple-violet, brown tinge.

(B) Fulton. 32 inches. Purple, gray bloom.

(B) Georges Grappe. 33 inches. Purple-violet.

(D) Insurpassable. 28 inches. Rosy lilac.

(B) Mrs. Beecher Stowe. 28 inches. Violet-purple.

(D) Queen of Night. 29 inches. Deep velvety maroon. Best of the very darks; surpasses La Tulipe Noire in quality.

(D) Scotch Lassie. 26 inches. Deep lilac.

PURPLE BLENDS

(B) Louis XIV. 30 inches. Violet flushed bronze and gold at edges. Old favorite.

(B) Mount Royal. Glowing bluish purple, edged bronze-orange.

(B) Rayburn. Violet edged bronze.

**Division 9. Lily-Flowered Tulips**

A group of Cottage Tulips with tapering tepals gracefully

reflexed. In a mixed border they add an airy touch to the groups of more formal tulips. They bloom with the other late tulips, and grow from about 24 to 30 inches. There is a good range of color.

Aladdin. 24 inches. Scarlet, edged pale yellow.
Astor. 26 inches. Soft blend of bronze, pink, and buff.
Captain Fryatt. 24 inches. Deep garnet red.
China Pink. 26 inches. Light pink, white base.
Crabeth. 26 inches. Bright rose-pink, paling to edges.
Elegans Alba (White Crown). 24 inches. White, narrow rose edges.
Fascinating. 26 inches. Creamy yellow.
Golden Duchess. 28 inches. Golden yellow.
Linette. 24 inches. Purple, white base.
Mariette. 29 inches. Bright satin rose-pink.
Maytime. 24 inches. Lilac, narrow white edge, base yellow.
Picotee. 24 inches. White, edged rose that gradually spreads over entire flower. Less attractive in this latter stage.
Red Shine. 29 inches. Clear deep red, blue center.
Sebastian. 26 inches. Deep golden yellow.
Stanislaus. 22 inches. Early for class. Bright orange-red.
The Bride. 26 inches. Cream-white.
White Triumphator. 28 inches. Pure white.

**Division 11. Rembrandt Tulips—Broken Darwin Tulips**

**Division 12. Bizarre Tulips—Broken Breeder and Cottage Tulips**

Single; striped or marked brown, bronze, "black," or purple on yellow ground.

**Division 13. Bijbloemen Tulips—Broken Breeder and Cottage Tulips**

Single; striped or marked rose, pink, violet, or purple on white ground.

These three classes of broken tulips represent the famous group so popular in Holland during the early seventeenth century, when they became the basis of reckless speculation. With only a few exceptions, they are the result of infection of standard solid-color tulips by one or more strains of virus. (*See* the article "Broken Tulips" by Professor E. van Slogteren in *The Daffodil and Tulip Year Book 1960* of the Royal Horticultural Society.)

In the home garden, the use of virus-infected tulips can easily result in the infection and breaking of the solid-colored kinds, and can also cause the infection of lilies. Aphids carry the virus from one flower to another. It is better to admire the broken tulips in the lovely old flower studies of the Dutch painters, where they are so often featured.

Those who long to try tulips of this type may grow the following few which resemble broken tulips, but are said to be true sports, not virus-infected. Two are classed as Rembrandts, and are sports of Darwins. Two are sports of Early Singles, the other a Greigii Hybrid (Division 19).

American Flag. (Rembrandt) 26 inches. Deep red and white stripes.

Cordell Hull. (Rembrandt) 24 inches. Deep red on white.

General de Wet. (Early Single) 15 inches. Bright orange and gold blend.

Pandour. (Greigii) 12 inches. Pale yellow, flamed with orange-red. Foliage mottled. Early.

Prince Carnaval. (Early Single) 15 inches. Golden yellow, flamed and feathered scarlet.

**Tulip Oddities**

Here are listed some varieties belonging to Divisions 6 through 10. Groups of two or three of them would add novelty to a planting, and they are interesting for flower arrangements.

Bond Street. (Cottage) 27 inches. Yellow, heavily edged orange.

Elegans Alba. (Lily Flowered) 24 inches. White, narrow rose edge which widens.

Inga Hume. (Cottage) 24 inches. Inside yellow, outside rose-red edged light yellow.

Magier. (Cottage) 27 inches. Opens white, edged violet; gradually suffused blue-violet.

Ossie Oswalda. (Cottage) 25 inches. Opens cream, faint rose on edges; color spreads until whole flower is rose.

Picotee. (Lily-Flowered) 24 inches. White, edged rose that gradually suffuses flower.

Queen of Spain. (Cottage) 27 inches. Deep cream, softly edged and feathered rose.

MORE THAN ONE FLOWER TO A STEM (all Cottage Tulips):

Bo-peep. Large flower at top, four or five smaller ones borne on lower branching stem. Pale yellow.

Georgette. 20 inches. Three or four flowers, soft yellow, narrow red edge.

Royal Command. Several good-sized bright red flowers to a stem.

Wallflower. 27 inches. Several flowers, wallflower red-brown, yellow base.

GREEN TULIPS (all Cottage Tulips):

Artist. 20 inches. Inside salmon rose, outside salmon rose with green stripe down each tepal. A little rumpled in form.

Greenland. 20 inches. Green, edged rose.

Viridiflora and its seedlings. Early for Cottage Tulip class. 18 inches. Feathered green outside. Colors range from white and yellows to red.

FRINGED TULIPS

Resemble Parrot Tulips, and are sometimes listed with them in catalogs.

Sundew. (Darwin) 28 inches. Cardinal red with fringed tepals.

The Skipper. (Breeder) 30 inches. A sport of 'Louis XIV.' Violet with fringed gold and bronze edges.

**Division 14. Parrot Tulips**

Tulips with tepals laciniated, often rather rumpled in form. Tall, May-flowering, except where noted.

Blue Parrot. 24 inches. Soft lilac-purple. Sport of 'Bleu Aimable.'

Fantasy. 27 inches. Salmon-pink, green markings outside. 'Clara Butt' sport.

Firebird. 27 inches. Brilliant red sport of 'Fantasy.'

Gemma. Sport of an Early Single, so short and early. White and soft pink.

Ivory Parrot. 24 inches. Creamy.

Orange Favorite. 24 inches. Bronzy orange, green markings. Yellow base.

Red Parrot. 30 inches. Dark raspberry red. Good stem.

Texas Gold. 24 inches. Deep yellow, narrow red edge.

Van Dyke. 28 inches. Deep rose-pink.

White Parrot. 24 inches. Pure white.

**Division 15. Late Double Tulips**

Full doubles, often listed as peony- or tree-peony-flowered. Bloom with other May-flowering tulips. Heights about 18 to 26 inches.

Coxa. 20 inches. Bright red, pale edges.

Eros. 22 inches. Old rose edged silver.

Gold Medal. 18 inches. Deep gold.

Lilac Perfection. 18 inches. Silvery lilac.

Mount Tacoma. 20 inches. Pure white.

Uncle Tom. 22 inches. Dark maroon-red.

The Divisions from 6 through 10, that is, Darwins and their hybrids, Breeders, Cottage, and Lily-Flowered Tulips are the ones that contribute the tall, smooth, stately flowers in a great range of colors that are so valued at the height of spring. The members of Divisions 11 through 15, often a little freakish in appearance, can be used in moderation to supplement them, but should not dominate the garden scene. The vast majority of the broken tulips of Divisions 11, 12 and 13, it is to be remembered, are infected with a virus.

The remaining Divisions from 16 to 22 were established to cover groups of hybrids and varieties that are now adding even more range (and confusion) to the array of tulips now available. The following species with their varieties and hybrids have been consigned to separate Divisions as here listed: 16. *T. batalinii;* 17. *T. eichleri;* 18. *T. fosteriana;* 19. *T. greigii;* 20. *T. kaufmanniana;* 21. *T. marjolettii;* 22. *T. tubergeniana.* 16, 17, 21 and 22 are not yet commercially important in this country.

Division 23 contains the remaining species and their varieties and hybrids (wild plants and hybrids in which the appearance of the wild plant is evident). Tulips in Divisions 16 to 23 are often listed in catalogs as "botanical tulips."

Many species tulips are natives of places with great extremes of climate, long, cold winters, and hot, dry summers. Those who live in the Northern Plains states would do well to try tulips whose ancestral homes are Turkestan, Bokhara, and northern Persia. They can be covered with six or eight inches of soil, even the little bulbs.

**Division 18. Fosteriana and its hybrids and varieties**

(*See also* Division 7, hybrids with Darwins.) Early-flowering.

Albas. 16 inches. White inside, dull rose outside.

Cantata. 8 inches. Bright orange-red, shiny bright green leaves. Later than 'Red Emperor.'

*T. fosteriana.* 12 to 18 inches. Turkestan. Very large brilliant red flowers. Early.

Golden Emperor. 16 inches. Golden yellow, early.

Intermezzo. 11 inches. Creamy yellow suffused pink.

Purissima (White Emperor). 16 inches. Opens creamy, turns pure white. Early, with 'Red Emperor.'

Red Emperor (Mme. Lefeber). 16 inches. Early, with Dutch crocuses. Brilliant red, inside base black bordered yellow.

Zombie. 16 inches. Outside bright rose edged apricot, inside yellow flushed rose. Early.

**Division 19. Greigii and its hybrids and varieties**

Early bloom, short stems, wavy mottled foliage.

*T. greigii.* 12 inches. Turkestan. Flowers orange-scarlet with dark yellow-margined base. Leaves broad, mottled with purple.

Mary Ann. 8 inches. Bright rose edged cream. Mid-spring.

Pandour. 12 inches. Pale yellow, flamed carmine red. Leaves mottled.

Red Riding Hood. 9 inches. Brilliant red small flowers. Mid-early.

Rockery Wonder. 10 inches. Flowers small, orange-bronze. Leaves mottled.

**Division 20. Kaufmanniana and its hybrids and varieties**

Early-flowering, with Dutch crocuses, many short-stemmed. Crosses with *T. greigii* give some varieties mottled foliage.

Alfred Cortot. 10 inches. Deep scarlet, black base. Leaves mottled.

César Franck. 10 inches. Outside scarlet edged gold, inside gold.

Gaiety. 6 inches. Creamy white, brushed rose outside.

*T. kaufmanniana,* Waterlily Tulip. 6 to 9 inches. Very dependable, and one of the prettiest. Turkestan. Creamy yellow, tepals brushed with rose on outside. Opens in sun into flat star, deeper yellow in center. Blooms with Dutch crocuses. Increases well. The first species to try.

Shakespeare. 7 inches. Inside salmon apricot, outside carmine-red edged salmon.

Vivaldi. 8 inches. Inside light yellow, outside carmine-rose edged yellow.

**Division 23. Remaining Species of Tulips and their varieties and hybrids in which the appearance of the wild plant is evident**

Also included here in this final list are *T. eichleri* (Division 17) and *T. marjolettii* (Division 21).

*Tulipa acuminata* (*T. cornuta; T. stenopetala*) Horned Tulip. 16 inches. Perhaps native of Turkey, perhaps of garden origin. Tepals very narrow, somewhat twisted. Red and yellow, opening out wide, spidery appearance.

*T. chrysantha* (by some considered a variety of *T. stellata*). 6 inches. Yellow flowers two inches across, suffused soft red outside. Starry. Persia to Kashmir. Mid-spring.

*T. clusiana,* Lady Tulip. 16 inches. Slender little flower. Inside white, outside striped crimson-pink on white. Early midseason. Not long-lasting in Northern states, but persists well where it is milder. Narrow leaves. Persia to Kashmir. Naturalized in southern Europe.

*T. dasystemon* (of gardens and catalogs), more properly *T. tarda*. 3 to 6 inches. One to six small starry flowers clustered on one stem. White tinged green outside, bright yellow within paling to edges. Early. From Turkestan.

*T. eichleri* (Division 17). 10 inches. Transcaucasia, Turkestan. Flowers medium size, bright orange-scarlet. Mid-early.

*T. linifolia*. 6 inches. Turkestan. Outside red softened with buff, inside bright scarlet-crimson. Opens flat. Narrow leaves. Early.

*T. marjolettii* (Division 21). 20 inches. Southern Europe. Creamy flowers edged rose. Late spring.

*T. praestans.* 12 inches. Turkestan. Several light red flowers to a stem. Early. Its variety 'Fusilier' has several rather small orange-scarlet flowers to a stem.

*T. primulina.* 8 inches. Mountains of Algeria. Starry white, brushed rose outside, one or two flowers to a stem.

*T. sprengeri.* 8 to 18 inches. Asia Minor. Deep red globular flowers very late in May.

*T. sylvestris,* Wood Tulip. 16 inches. Europe, North Africa, to Persia. Golden yellow, tepals recurved, outer ones brushed brown or green, fragrant. Sometimes two flowers to a stem. Midseason. It increases by stolons in deep, good soil. (A stolon is a horizontal stem on or under the ground that produces a new plant at its tip.)

*T. turkestanica.* 8 inches. Very early (March) starry flowers, several to a stem. They are about 1½ inches across, white with a yellow blotch inside, tinged brown outside. A sturdy tetraploid.

Other species are commonly offered in catalogs. The small tulips are lovely rock-garden subjects, and vary from garden to garden in their reliability after the first year. Very good drainage should be given them. They should not be crowded by other plants while they are ripening their foliage, and should be in places where they will not get extra water during their dormant season.

If they are planted with other drought-resistant material, there will be no reason to give them more water than nature provides. Among the smaller sedums there is a wide variety of foliage and flower, and a planting of interest and beauty can be made of them alone. Antennarias and sempervivums can also be used.

## TULIPS IN THE GARDEN PICTURE

Care and judgment concerning their colors must be used in placing tulips about the home grounds. Tulips may make scenes of outstanding beauty, or they may make garish ones.

The wisest choices are often the simplest ones. First point to be considered is the color of the house itself. Many houses these days are painted shades of pinks, salmons, turquoise, blues, and greens that were unknown as house colors a few years ago. Awning colors are often factors to be considered. Brick varies in its hue. Sometimes brick houses are difficult, sometimes wonderful foils for flower colors.

Consider also the permanent plantings about the house. Have you many red azaleas? Red Japanese maples? With these consider white tulips, as white is a strong color, or cream. If you long for red tulips, too, use the early 'Red Emperor' or 'Couleur Cardinal,' which will bloom before the others are far advanced.

Against evergreens, you may use the brilliant orange-reds or flaming scarlets. Underplant them with lavender-blue *Phlox divaricata,* or edge them with blue or white pansies, or with the long-lasting double white arabis.

You can plan for a succession of color effects. That is better than trying to have everything all at once. You might try the difficult and most brilliant colors for an early show, leading in mid-spring into the gentler pinks, roses, yellows, and deep maroons of Darwin and Cottage varieties. These can be combined beautifully with the evergreen azaleas in many colors and with early perennials.

Perhaps you prefer the bronze, terra cotta, and purple blends to be found among the Breeders. If so, forget pink and rose. Include light and golden yellows, and add the yellow, blue, and blue-lavender of other plant material. The result will be striking and harmonious.

Tulips in groups of less than ten are apt to be ineffective. Fifteen to twenty-five in a group make good masses among perennials in a mixed border.

The same varieties may be repeated at intervals, or similar colors may be repeated in different varieties, which gives you a chance to become acquainted with more kinds.

BRIDGES IN COLOR. White is the most obvious way to separate two colors that would otherwise look too nearly alike, or that would not look well together. But a mass of white in the garden is very insistent, and so often a peacemaker that is softer in effect, such as light yellow or cream, is a better choice. Deep colors such as wine red and maroons or violets are also good bridges. Kinds that are blends of two or more colors also are very helpful. Select a range of pale, medium, and dark varieties.

MIXED TULIPS. The commercial tulip mixtures of all colors are not effective for garden decoration, but may be useful in the cutting garden. However, special mixtures can be used effectively. I remember a Virginia garden in which the box-edged beds were filled with intermingled white, silvery lilac, and purple-violet tulips. On one side was a wall of mellow brick. Box planted along its base gave a green background for the tulips. A wisteria had been trained to trail lavender clusters down over the top edge of the brick above the tulips. From this garden one strolled into another, divided from it, but only partially concealed, by a few large box bushes. In this garden, the beds were planted with mixed tulips in bright red and soft yellow.

In a Pennsylvania garden, formal beds were filled with white tulips. Other color was supplied by tree wisterias and pink and white dogwoods. On another place, an unexpected gift of a hundred red tulips was used in front of the foundation planting of a white house. There was an edging of white pansies in front of the tulips. Simple and effective.

A FEW COLOR COMBINATIONS. With forsythia—early tulips, single and double, in yellow, terra cotta, and orange. Add some bright blue squills. Daffodils, early bulbous iris, and pansies, blue to blue-violet, are other possibilities.

With azaleas—the evergreen azaleas in pinks and reds and tulips in soft yellows, in pinks, roses, and crimsons can be used well together. Plenty of light colors and soft tints are needed. The fewer the colors used, the more carefully must they be selected for a pleasing result.

Azaleas in salmon, brick reds, and orange-red can be combined with creams, soft yellows, and blended salmons of tulips. If a certain group of tulips turns out to have been a mistake, it can always be used to supply cut flowers for the house. It is often the lilac-pinks that cause grief in these combinations.

With lilacs—salmon and yellow tulips look well with the single blue-violet 'Decaisne' and double 'Olivier de Serres.' Pink and rose tulips combine beautifully with such pink lilacs as 'Belle de Nancy,' 'Mme. Antoine Buchner,' 'Esther Staley,' and the graceful *Syringa microphylla superba*.

Lilacs of lilac color can be accompanied by tulips in white, lilacs, and purples, and the same ones are striking with deep purple lilacs such as 'Night,' 'Ludwig Spaeth,' and 'Mrs. W. E. Marshall.'

Rose bed—young rose foliage contains much beautiful copper and gold. An edging of blue grape-hyacinths gives spring interest. There might also be room for a few groups of the Single Early Tulips 'General de Wet' (orange and gold blend) and yellow 'Rising Sun.'

The graceful arching sprays of the large bleeding-heart

(*Dicentra spectabilis*), the blue-lavender *Phlox divaricata,* pansies, hardy candytuft, English daisies in pink and white, dwarf bearded iris, and a wealth of other bulbous material combined with the early spring shrubs such as azaleas, low deutzias, bridalwreath, and other spireas offer endless possibilities, combined with the colors of the tulip, to suit all tastes. The combinations can be in pastels and muted colors, or dazzling in their brilliance, simple or complicated. But they deserve some thought, and usually modifications from time to time. Painting pictures with the tulip's colors is an occupation to last a lifetime.

CHAPTER VII

# Bulbs for Late Spring and Early Summer

By the time spring is at its height, there is so much bloom from shrubs and trees as well as herbaceous plants that the choice of what bulbs to plant becomes harder. Or perhaps it really becomes easier, for what can compete with the daffodils and tulips? But some of the late spring bulbs can be used to supplement and accentuate the beauty of those important flowers. The tall scillas, for example, and mertensia, camassia, and *Ornithogalum nutans* serve well in this way, although each has also its own particular loveliness.

The versatile ornamental onions can play a variety of roles, and if they are not quite up to playing star, at least they can give valuable support. Scillas and mertensias are especially useful for naturalizing, and some of the onions, too, adapt themselves to a wild situation.

But the tall bulbous iris, with their clear, strong colors and dignified carriage, deserve to be featured.

## TALL BULBOUS IRIS

There are three groups of tall, bulbous iris that are commonly grown: the Dutch, Spanish, and English iris. All are of garden origin, and are derived from species native to Spain, Portugal, and northern Africa. The Dutch and Spanish iris, both derived from *Iris xiphium,* require sharp drainage and summer heat in soil that is rather dry and preferably sandy. The English iris, descended from *Iris xiphioides,* a species from the cool, moist meadows of the Pyrenees, need cool, rather moist soil in the garden.

The flowers of these groups, like those of the early bulbous iris, are beardless. Instead of a patch of hairs, they have a smooth patch or stripe of yellow in the center of each fall. (The falls are the three lower, drooping segments of the flower.)

The bulbs, which are enclosed by membranous tunics, should be planted with about three inches of soil over them, and about five or six inches apart.

The tall bulbous iris are good for garden massing much like the tall late tulips. Like tulips, when they have played their part in the garden picture they can be removed to give room for annuals. In this respect, the Dutch varieties have an advantage since they bloom earlier. But Spanish iris extend the season, and are especially useful where there is room for a cutting garden.

The Dutch and Spanish iris can be lifted after blooming and ripening, and stored until fall planting time. Where summer rains are plentiful, this is especially desirable. In warm, dry parts of the country (such as California) they grow extremely well. In the East, they are apt to peter out in a few years, as tulips do. However, they are not expensive, and where they are satisfactory garden plants, replacements are not a serious matter.

DUTCH IRIS. This is the earliest group to bloom, appearing with the tall bearded iris, or just following them. The well-known blue iris of florist shops, 'Wedgwood,' is a good example of the general appearance of the members of this group. The colors are rich and varied, ranging from white, yellow, and bronze to blue, violet, and lilac. Sometimes blue and bronze are combined in the same flower.

In the warmer states, the Dutch iris are very satisfactory, but in the North, the many kinds of non-bulbous iris give results that are much better. The bulbs of Dutch iris send up their foliage in the fall, and late planting is desirable to hold it back as much as possible. After the top surface of the ground is frozen, they should be covered with a deep but open mulch.

The following varieties give a good idea of the color range. All reach a height of about 2 feet, and bear one or two flowers to a stem. The slender, graceful leaves do not reach the height of the flowers.

Blue Champion. Large clear blue; gold blotch in center of falls.

Blue Triumphator. Muted gray-blue; yellow stripe down middle of each fall.

Bronze Queen. Standards (the three upper segments) blue blended bronze; falls (the three lower segments) rich bronze with large yellow blotches.

Golden Harvest. Rich yellow.

Harmony. Lavender-blue standards; falls soft yellow with orange blotch.

Jeanne d'Arc. Tall, large-flowered creamy white.

Lemon Queen. Standards palest yellow; falls a little deeper.

Pride of Holland. Deep golden yellow.

Princess Irene. Standards white; falls bright golden orange.

White Excelsior. Late large pure white.

SPANISH IRIS. This group blooms about two weeks after the Dutch iris, and requires the same culture: plenty of sun, and a light, well-drained soil. Late planting and a winter mulch to protect the foliage from cold are necessary.

The foliage and flowers are a little smaller than those of the Dutch iris. The plants reach about 18 inches in height. They lack the vigor of the Dutch group, but have almost the same color range.

Cajanus. Clear yellow; gold blotch on falls.

Excelsior. Light violet-blue.
King of the Blues. Deep blue with small yellow blotch.
Hercules. Standards purplish-blue shaded bronze; falls golden bronze, gold blotch.
L'Innocence. Late pure white.
Le Mogul. Bronze; gold blotch on falls.

ENGLISH IRIS. Colors in this group run from pale to dark blues, lilac-pink to red-purple and blue-purple, white and bicolors. The flowers have a look of elegance compared with the gaudier Dutch iris. They bloom toward the end of June. They require a moister location than the Dutch and Spanish varieties, and a cooler summer climate. In some places along the eastern seaboard, as far north as Maine, in slightly damp locations tempered summer and winter by the sea, they sometimes last for many years. As they form clumps, they must be divided and reset. However, usually they need replacements after a few years. The plants do not make any fall growth, but should have a winter mulch.

Disease: English iris are often infected with one of the viruses that cause color breaking in tulips, and this causes stunting of the plants and dark mottling of the flowers. Virus-free seedlings are offered by some American dealers. Although the colors are mixed, all blend together harmoniously. Since the virus can be spread between iris and tulips by aphids, it seems unwise to take a chance on named varieties. Any that show mottling should be destroyed.

## TALL SCILLAS

The Spanish and English bluebells or wood-hyacinths labor under the disadvantage of too many names, none of which is well known to the average gardener, who may know them by sight without knowing any name by which to identify them. They moved from *Hyacinthus* to *Scilla,* where they have been

## Bulbs for Late Spring and Early Summer

for some time, and now have been moved back to another older name, *Endymion*. Who knows for how long? Surely they will continue as scillas in commerce for a long time. The smaller species of scillas, sometimes known as squills (*see* Chapter III), remain in the genus *Scilla*.

These bluebells resemble hyacinths, but with few flowers on a scape. They may be had in clear lavender-blues, lavenders, lilac-pinks, and white. They are at their best in the blue range, but their coloring is always soft, never as intense as that of the Dutch hyacinths.

They are long-lived, increasing into clumps with many spires of bloom, and if the soil is reasonably good, will endure considerable shade, an especially valuable characteristic. They can be planted in masses, or grouped with ferns and other shade-loving plants. The blue varieties are best for naturalizing, but the pinks and whites can be used in clumps of six or a dozen effectively planted with other things. Since the pinks all have a touch of lilac in them, their color is best kept away from the pure pinks of other flowers, which make them look washed out and faded.

The bulbs should be covered with three or four inches of soil, and planted five to six or ten to twelve inches apart, depending on how immediate an effect is wanted.

*Scilla hispanica* (*Endymion hispanicus, Scilla campanulata*), Spanish Bluebell. The scape, which reaches 12 to 15 inches or more, is hung with ten to twenty bell-shaped flowers about ¾ inch long. The numerous leaves are about eight inches long and ½ inch wide. The flowering season is just before the late tulips in this area, but farther north, where spring is shorter, they bloom together. The Spanish bluebell, taller and showier, is a better garden plant than its English counterpart.

Excelsior. Tall, with large deep lavender-blue bells. Very fine.

Myosotis. Large spikes of clear lavender-blue, a color that usually passes for blue in describing flower colors.

Rosabella. Soft pale pink.

Rose Queen. Rosy pink.

White Triumphator. Tall spikes.

*Scilla nonscripta* (*E. nonscriptus, S. nutans*), English Bluebell. The flower of the famous English bluebell woods, not to be confused with the Scotch bluebell or harebell (*Campanula rotundifolia*), which is not bulbous. Leaves a little narrower, and flowers a little more tubular than the Spanish bluebell. There are blue, pink, and white varieties.

## MERTENSIA

Another of the plants called bluebells. A genus of the Borage Family, and thereby closely related to forget-me-nots and pulmonarias. About forty species of the Northern Hemisphere, one a popular garden plant.

*Mertensia virginica,* Virginia Bluebells, Virginia Cowslip. Clusters of pink buds open into nodding sky-blue bells about an inch long, on leafy stalks 18 to 24 inches high, in mid-spring. One of the loveliest blues available for the garden, and one of the nearest to a true blue. The thickened tuberous roots are often marketed in a dormant condition like bulbs, and should be planted as soon as they are obtained. The ground should be watered if it is dry. Cover with three inches of soil.

In wild and semi-wild situations, mertensia seeds itself freely. It should have a soil rich in humus that does not dry out. It is a splendid spring flower to accompany tulips in light shade. Since the foliage disappears in early summer, mertensia must be planted in a place where the resulting bare ground does not matter, or where other plants will fill in over it.

## THE ALLIUMS

The alliums are onions, and far more intriguing as garden ornaments than that statement suggests. The genus, containing about 500 species found throughout the Northern Hemisphere, belongs to the Lily Family. In addition to the ones so valued in cookery, there are several dozen that are prized by gardeners who have become acquainted with their varied charms.

They range from a few inches in height to over four feet; in color, from whites to pinks, blues, yellows, lavenders, and lilacs to rich, glowing purples. The flowers are small, but borne in many-flowered umbels, each flower on its own little stalk or *pedicel* branching out from a common point, like the ribs of an umbrella. In a few species, the thick-set flowers make a ball-shaped inflorescence; in others, the flower head is domed, but not completely round. Some have flowers on pedicels of unequal length, which give the effect of a bursting skyrocket as they open, and there are those which have just a few bells or stars at the top of the scape. Many have leaves that are narrow or almost grassy; the leaves of others are quite broad. The typical onion smell is apparent only when the leaves are bruized. The flowers of some kinds are delightfully fragrant.

The large ball alliums are really quite extraordinary. Even one bulb is worth planting. Some are inexpensive, but others cost a dollar or two for one bulb. A few of the tall ones grouped to make an accent among perennials are striking. The foliage of all discussed here, except three, dies away quickly as soon as they have finished flowering.

The bulbs of some species are so slender that it is impractical to handle them in a dry and dormant condition, separated from the clustered mass in which they naturally grow, so these species, and the very small ones as well, must be grown from seed or secured as plants. Other species make good firm bulbs, some of them of considerable size. The seed gathered from species growing near other species that bloom at the same time may be unsatisfactory. It is apt to result in hybrids that have lost the distinctive characteristics of the parents and gained nothing in return.

Most alliums are hardy, and require only the average properly tended and well-drained garden soil and a fair to good amount of sun. Rate of increase varies. Some divide and set seed readily, others increase very slowly. It is well to keep a watch for seedlings, for some may like your garden so well that they will start to take over. Better to start curbing them before they have spread very far by removing faded flower heads.

On the whole, the alliums are not a fussy group. It must also be admitted that many are not very interesting. But the choicest of them are so attractive that they deserve far more attention from gardeners than they get. The ones listed here give a good range of colors, forms, and season, and are among the best offered as dormant bulbs.

*Allium schoenoprasum,* Chives. Since this is easily obtained, useful, and an attractive garden plant, it is listed first. Two or three of the small pots of forced chives found in late winter in food markets can be kept watered in a sunny window until spring, and then set out. The heads of rosy purple flowers, about ¾ of an inch across, on scapes 8 or 10 inches high, appear in late spring. After two or three years, the clumps will be thick enough to need dividing to maintain good growth. When cutting the leaves for kitchen use, take a small portion of the foliage all the way to the ground, instead of just trimming off an inch or so of the tops over a larger part of the clump. The plant is green until cold weather.

The following kinds are procurable as bulbs in the autumn, and should be covered with a depth of soil equal to their own depth, and at distances apart suitable for the size of their flower heads.

*A. aflatunense.* 30 to 36 inches. Produces in late spring a rather loose ball four to six inches across of stars that are a pleasant, strong purple-violet. The leaves are about four inches wide. Plant six to eight inches apart.

*A. albopilosum,* Stars of Persia. 24 to 30 inches. Stars, pale violet with a silver sheen, in domed clusters eight or more inches across, open in early summer. It is hardy in the Philadelphia area, but is safer planted six inches deep and mulched here and

## Bulbs for Late Spring and Early Summer

to the north. It is among the most effective and interesting of the alliums. Plant eight to twelve inches apart.

*A. caeruleum* (usually listed as *A. azureum*). 18 to 30 inches. The starry flowers in heads two inches across are a very pretty blue, just moderately tinted with violet, and stay in good condition a long time in early summer. The leaves are narrow. It is a dainty plant that needs contrasting color to show up to best advantage. Bulbils that appear in the flower clusters may be gathered as the flower stems dry up and planted to start growing on to blooming size. Plant four to six inches apart.

*A. elatum.* 30 to 36 inches. This bears starry flowers of a rather insipid lilac-rose in late spring. The broad leaves are about a foot long and four inches across. Plant six to eight inches apart.

*A. flavum.* 18 inches. The slender pyramid of buds opens into a skyrocket of golden bells in midsummer. The fine leaves are cylindrical, and green all summer. Plant four to six inches apart.

*A. giganteum.* 48 to 60 inches. The ball of rich purple stars is four or five inches across in early summer. The bulb, too, is a giant. Plant eight to ten inches apart.

*A. karataviense.* 8 to 15 inches. This allium opens as the last tulips are beginning to fade. The flower head is filled with white stars veined with purple or pink, and is about three inches across. It is not quite a full ball. It rises above three broad blue-green leaves that are finely edged with red. The leaves make an important contribution to the soft, subtle beauty of this species. Plant five to seven inches apart.

*A. moly,* Golden Garlic, Lily Leek. 8 to 12 inches. Bright yellow stars in loose heads about three inches across appear in early summer. The gray-green leaves are about an inch across. Plant four to six inches apart.

*A. neapolitanum,* Naples Onion. To 12 inches. The fragrant starry white flowers are borne in loose umbels about three inches across in mid-spring. The leaves are about an inch wide. It is not reliably hardy. Except in the South, it needs a sheltered place and a mulch.

*A. oreophilum ostrowskyanum.* 8 to 16 inches. The three-inch ball of pink or purple stars opens in late spring. The leaves are narrow and gray-green. There is a deep rosy-red variety called 'Zwanenburg.' The colors are clear, bright, and attractive, and look well together. Plant four to six inches apart.

*A. pulchellum.* To 18 inches. The loose umbel of rosy lilac opens in a graceful skyrocket in late spring, but occasional umbels may appear later. Delicate and charming in appearance. The rounded leaves stay green until fall.

## CAMASSIA (CAMASS)

A small genus of half a dozen bulbous plants of the Lily Family, native to North America, all but one in the West, and once an important food of the Indians. The delicate, starry flowers are set all about the tall scape, making a graceful spire.

Camassias grow in rich meadows which have plenty of moisture, at least in spring. They are not for hot, dry locations. The stalks are not always as stiff in gardens as one could wish, and may require support.

They can be planted in clumps of six or eight in the mixed border, where they will bloom with the tulips. They should be left undisturbed to establish themselves, which may take three or four years. Plant nine or ten inches apart, cover four inches, in good soil that does not dry out.

*Camassia quamash,* Common Camass. Sometimes listed as *C. esculenta.* 2 to 3 feet. White to lavender-blue, but the lavender-blue form is the one most generally in commerce.

*C. leichtlini.* 3 feet or more. The best for cultivation. From dark lavender-blue to white, many flowers in a spire. They are sold according to color. The white form is especially lovely.

## ORNITHOGALUM

About a hundred species of bulbous plants of the Old World belonging to the Lily Family. *O. umbellatum,* the star-of-Bethlehem, widely naturalized in the East, forms thick tufts of crocus-like foliage, often with little or no bloom. The starry flowers, white, and about an inch across on 6-inch scapes, open only in sun and close at noon. At its best, it is a pretty thing, but it can also be an unwelcome intruder in gardens where the space might better be occupied by better plants. There seems to be evidence that it can also harbor viruses that affect lilies.

*Ornithogalum nutans,* Nodding Star-of-Bethlehem. This is also naturalized in meadows and along roadsides in some places in the East. It is modest and pretty, growing about 18 inches high with flowers about two inches across, silvery white inside and green edged silver outside. A few at the edge of a woodland, or in a semi-wild place with some sun and not too dry, are attractive with some low ferns. The tunicated bulbs can be covered with about four inches of soil, and planted four to five inches apart.

# CHAPTER VIII

# Lilies

Lilies, those beautiful and tantalizing flowers, have long been the joy and the despair of gardeners. They have been inconstant and inconsistent creatures, flourishing without any particular care in some gardens, pining away and disappearing in others. Now that so much is known about the reasons for their erratic behavior and how to deal with it, we should look forward to an increasing use of this splendid genus.

With their diversified shapes, their long season of bloom, their wide range of handsome colors and variations in plant height, lilies should play an important role in the garden. Many are very fragrant, too, and that is no mean gift.

### THE GENUS LILIUM

Lilies form the genus *Lilium,* and impart their name to the Lily Family or *Liliaceae.* There are eighty or more species in the genus, all found in the North Temperate zone. They have close relatives such as the daylilies (*Hemerocallis*) and lily-of-the-valley which also belong to the Lily Family but not to the genus *Lilium.* Their name has also been borrowed to form the names of such unrelated plants as the waterlily.

True lilies have scaly bulbs and upright, leafy stems. Among them are several general types of flowers, which can be roughly

Turkscap lily. Many species and varieties of lily have drooping or pendent flowers with tepals slightly to strongly reflexed.

grouped according to shape. There are the trumpets, shaped like Easter lilies, and probably the kind that comes into the minds of most people when lilies are mentioned. Another group has flowers of the Turkscap type, usually rather drooping, with the six tepals recurved. Some hold their flowers upright like cups, and the flowers of these may be almost starry, or with broad, widely flaring, but not reflexed tepals. A variation of the cup or bowl shape is the rather flat-faced flower which faces sideways, or droops a little.

The flood of new lily hybrids of the last twenty-five years has brought many gradations between trumpets, Turkscaps, bowls, and stars. But as far as garden use goes, it is helpful to bear in mind the range of shapes when decisions are being made on what lilies to buy.

In colors, there are whites, yellows, oranges, apricots, scarlets, pinks, crimsons, purples, lilacs, and deep maroons. Some flowers are a deeper color outside; some are pleasingly spotted. Bloom-

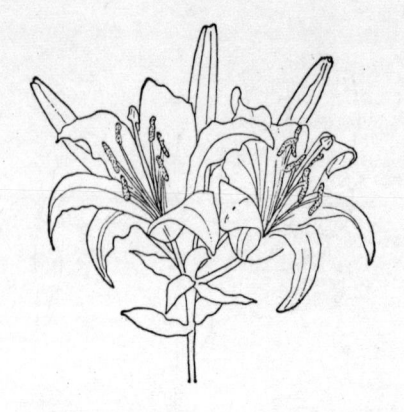

Upward-facing lilies may be bowl-shaped or starry.

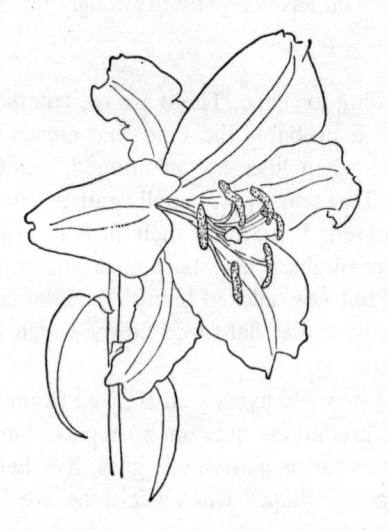

Bowl-shaped lilies are widely open, and face upward or sideways. Tepals are flaring, and may be partly reflexed.

ing time stretches from late spring or early summer to early fall. Size varies from flowers with tepals a little over an inch long to those whose entire diameter nears a foot. In height, the range is from a foot to 6 or 7 feet.

BECOMING ACQUAINTED WITH LILIES. It takes reading, asking, and trying to gain the knowledge necessary for success with lilies.

First, forget for a while the lilies with the old familiar names, such as the madonna lily (*L. candidum*), the goldband lily (*L. auratum*) and *Lilium speciosum,* with its reflexed blooms of pink and crimson. Forget even the regal lily (*L. regale*).

The tepals of trumpet lilies overlap for most of their length, flaring out at the mouth.

Begin with a few of the new, easily obtained hybrid groups. Second, if you really want to know how to grow lilies, watch the garden magazines for announcements of lily shows near you. Go to a show. Talk with the lily growers, who will be mostly amateurs, to learn something of local problems. Third, join the North American Lily Society. Its splendid yearbooks and bulletins are a continuing source of information on the latest in the world of lily enthusiasts. The general garden magazines cannot present fully the wealth of information that is published year after year by the society.

## BUYING AND PLANTING LILIES

Lily bulbs are more vulnerable than those of daffodils and tulips. They lack the protection of a dry tunic. Rough handling may bruise them or break off scales, and exposure to the air may dry them out. They should be harvested and shipped with the roots intact, and these roots should be protected from drying. The lily does not take kindly to being treated as a dormant plant.

Do not buy bulbs that are rootless, shriveled, or have unhealthy-looking scales, perhaps with brown patches on them. If you buy species, ascertain their origin, and be sure they are healthy to begin with. A healthy bulb is more of a bargain than a cheap bulb, even if it costs more. There are a number of nurseries specializing in lilies, and it is their pride to offer the best. If bulbs arrive looking a little shriveled, plump them up for a few days in moist sand or peat moss. But they should be planted as soon as possible.

SOIL AND SITE REQUIREMENTS. Like other bulbs, lilies require good drainage, only their need for it is more acute, especially in the garden. At the same time, they should have a soil well supplied with humus, slightly acid to neutral for most of them. They should have good air circulation, but be sheltered from the stronger winds that prevail at the time they are in bloom.

Mulches help them winter and summer, preserving moisture, keeping soil temperatures as constant as possible, and lightening the task of weeding and cultivating. In spring this is especially important, for lilies are often late to appear, and do not always emerge from the soil just where you think they should. Cultivation can be dangerous to those precious shoots.

Because of the danger of basal rot, manures should be avoided, and fertilizers low in nitrogen should be used. Where summers are consistently dry and where lilies can be planted in fresh soil, basal rot may be less of a threat, but in the humid states it is always to be feared, and there is no use in tempting Providence, even when resistant lilies are being grown.

TIME AND DEPTH OF PLANTING. Most lilies should be planted as soon as they can be obtained in the fall, which is not likely to be before soils have cooled off somewhat. The madonna lily (*L. candidum*) is a notable exception. It should be planted in August or early September so that it will have time to produce its fall rosette of leaves.

If late delivery of bulbs is likely, the holes should be prepared in advance, and protected against freezing with a mulch.

Most lilies produce roots not only from the base of the bulbs, but along the stem from the top of the bulb to the surface of the soil. Others root only from the base of the bulb. Stem-rooting lilies should be covered with four to six inches of soil, perhaps a little more if the soil is quite sandy. The madonna lily should be covered with one to two inches, and other base-rooting kinds just a little deeper. The ones without stem roots most likely to be tried by the average gardener are the madonna lily (*L. candidum*), the martagon (*L. martagon*), and American Turkscap (*L. superbum*).

HOW TO PLANT. Before they are planted, the bulbs should be dusted with Arasan or Spergon. A little of the dust is shaken into a bag with the bulbs, the bag closed and turned over and over so that the bulbs are thoroughly coated. Wear gloves while handling coated bulbs. Those willing to take more trouble may soak the bulbs for fifteen minutes in a saturated solution of Tersan (two ounces in a gallon of water).

The hole for a lily bulb must be large enough to accommodate the roots without crowding. In accordance with what has been said before, the soil should have been prepared to the depth needed for all-around satisfactory good gardening with bulbs—at least a foot deep, and with particular attention to good drainage. The bulb is placed in the hole, and soil worked in around the roots so that no air spaces are left. The soil should be moist enough to prevent drying out of the roots and bulb after planting.

If the lily is one that grows tall, it can be marked with a stake at planting time. Low lilies should also be marked in some way so their locations will be known. Although growing shoots often appear aboveground a little distance away from the bulb, markers are needed as guides to prevent injuries.

Most lilies should be placed about a foot apart to allow room for the spread of the flower clusters. The largest and tallest could be given a few inches more, for a fine stalk of lilies in bloom is more effective if it is not jostled by its neighbors.

MULCHING. After the surface of the ground has frozen, a mulch can be put on. It will maintain more even soil temperatures during the winter, and in spring will hold back for a while the sprouts of some of the frost-sensitive kinds.

The mulch can be left on all year round, with material being added as it decays, but the relation of mulches to rodents must be remembered. If mice are a problem, the mulch might better be removed in the fall and left off until the ground has frozen for an inch or two.

## ROUTINE CARE

Spring care of lilies consists of leaving them alone. The young shoots are erratic about appearing, and easily broken. If there is a mulch, there is no need to cultivate, but if there is no mulch, when the shoots are well up, the surface can be cultivated, but the job must be done lightly so that the stem roots are not damaged. When the shoots are about 6 inches high, they should have their first spray of Bordeaux (*see* page 143).

Lilies that need staking should be tied up before the buds have developed very far. A clump of many stems is better served by three or four stakes placed around it. Then there can be a sort of net of supporting string which will hold the stems fairly upright without destroying their natural grace.

Remember that cutting lilies for the house destroys at least part of the foliage, and thereby starves the bulbs to whatever extent the foliage is removed. For permanence and increase, resist that impulse. If temptation is too great, cut only the top third of the stem.

After the flowers have faded, they should be cut off to prevent seed formation. If seed is wanted, only one or two pods should be left to develop. Do not cut off any foliage until it has turned yellow and is starting to brown. Then the stalk can be cut off close to the ground, and removed with all foliage, and burned.

BULBLETS AND BULBILS. Lilies can be increased by division, by a process called *scaling,* by the *bulblets* produced on the underground part of the stem, and by the *bulbils* which are produced by some kinds in the leaf axils.

Bulblets can be removed from the lower flower stems in early fall and transferred to a small nursery bed where they are kept for a year or two. The bulbils are removed from the upper stem when they are mature enough to come off easily, and planted in the nursery. These small bulbs should be covered with an inch of soil and a mulch to prevent winter heaving. Their own roots have the ability to pull them down to a lower depth after their first year's growth.

Scaling is a process in which scales are removed from mature bulbs and induced to produce bulblets, but this is a procedure best left to experienced gardeners.

When lilies increase naturally by division, leave them alone until the clump is really crowded. When dividing becomes necessary, the bulbs should be taken up, separated, and replanted immediately. It can be done in early summer after the shoots have passed the most brittle stage, or in the fall when the foliage has turned yellow.

Only virus-free, healthy plants should be used for asexual propagation (using bulbils, bulblets, or division), as the virus will be carried into the new plants from diseased parents.

## PESTS AND DISEASES

Lilies have long been considered difficult to grow, but it was not until the development of modern plant pathology that the reasons for the difficulties were ferreted out. In 1920 the virus which causes lily mosaic was discovered. While that time seems like the dark ages to those born since, it is not long ago in terms of coming to realize the extent of the problem and learning how to cope with it. How far have we gotten in learning to cope with the virus of the common cold?

While lilies in the wild continue healthy year after year, cultural and marketing practices fostered the spread of diseases in lilies to such an extent that whole stocks were infected. Lilies might flourish in gardens for years, only to perish when they were infected by new lilies planted near them.

Since virus diseases of lilies are not transmitted through seed, the first step was to turn to growing clean stocks of the species. The next was to start, through breeding and selection, to develop plants tolerant and resistant to disease. While results of these programs are now available, surely the future will bring even healthier plants which have gained further beauty.

A perusal of the membership list of the North American Lily Society reveals that the majority of members live in the cooler states and Canada, some of them in very cold climates. This is an indication of the hardiness of lilies with proper mulching. But there is another significant aspect of the meager membership in the warmer states. That is the relationship between the basal rot of lilies and warm soils.

BASAL ROT. Professor George L. Slate of the New York Agricultural Experiment Station, Geneva, New York, who has made the growing of lilies a lifetime hobby, has summed up the lily disease problem as it now exists in two short, thorough articles in the 1959 and 1962 yearbooks of the North American Lily Society. He has come to believe that basal rot, caused by a fusarium which is related to that which causes basal rot in daffodils, is the most serious disease of lilies. It lives on in the soil for many years after its victims have disappeared. It can be tracked through the garden on shoes, and presumably on tools.

Only bulbs completely healthy in appearance should be planted. Any with traces of brown rot at the base of the scales should be discarded. Dust the bulbs to be planted with Arasan or Spergon. Do not use organic fertilizers. In choosing chemical fertilizers, pick the ones low in nitrogen. Possible formulas are 5-10-10 and 4-10-6. Be sure that drainage is of the best—quick and complete. If susceptible lilies are to be grown, building a raised bed is an added insurance of good drainage.

Although basal rot is less of a problem in areas where soils stay rather cool in summer, no garden can be considered immune. Dr. Slate believes that sooner or later the garden where lilies are grown will have fusarium rot. Then the gardener must turn to resistant lilies, or resort to soil fumigation, an unpleasant and toilsome procedure. He considers chloropicrin, sold under the name of Larvacide, the best fumigating material for fusarium, used according to the manufacturer's directions. Of course only disease-free bulbs should be planted in the sterilized soil.

Basal rot often shows up in growing plants with stunted growth and prematurely yellowing foliage, but sometimes the plants can maintain themselves through the summer by means of the stem roots, while the bulb is decaying. Then it simply does not appear the next spring.

Susceptible species include: *auratum, candidum, cernuum, formosanum, japonicum, rubellum, testaceum, willmottiae,* and some of its hybrids, including the Stenographer Series.

Lilies showing resistance include: Aurelian hybrids, *canadense, hansonii,* Mid-Century Hybrids, *speciosum,* and *superbum.*

VIRUSES. Among the viruses to which lilies are prone is the lily mosaic, a strain of the cucumber mosaic, but a different one from that which attacks daffodils. The lily mosaic also attacks fritillarias, which are closely related to lilies. Star-of-Bethlehem (*Ornithogalum umbellatum*), a small bulb which may be planted in gardens or be present as a weed, is likewise susceptible, and might best be eliminated from gardens where lilies are wanted.

There are other viruses which attack tulips as well as lilies, causing striping or blotching in otherwise solid-color tulip flowers. Any affected tulips that appear should be removed and burned immediately. Viruses tend to be more serious if present in combination than if they occur separately.

The virus which affects tobacco, tomatoes, and petunias, and which can be transmitted by smokers to those plants, does not affect lilies.

The mosaic causes a mottling of light and dark green in the foliage, which is sometimes distorted as well. Sometimes the mottling is in long, light streaks, as in *auratum, canadense, speciosum,* and *superbum.* In most lilies it appears as a pattern of light and dark blotches. Sometimes the plants are dwarfed, and the leaves die prematurely, starting from the base and progressing up the stem. Flowers may be poor in color and distorted. An iron deficiency may also cause mottling, but the veins remain green so that a rather regular pattern is formed.

As with daffodils, the mosaic is easier to discern early in the season. By summer, it is apt to be masked, unless the plant is very sick. The gardener who is aiming for a mosaic-free garden should promptly dig out and burn plants showing symptoms, as there is no cure. If one part of the garden is to be kept pure, but Typhoid Marys are allowed in another part, there should be at least 300 feet between the two, preferably with a building to act as an aphid barrier, for lily mosaic can be transmitted by aphids and other sucking insects.

Lilies resistant to viruses are *martagon* and *hansonii* and their hybrids. Lilies tolerant of viruses include: Aurelian hybrids, Mid-Century Hybrids, *testaceum,* and *tigrinum. L. speciosum* is tolerant to a moderate extent.

Among the lilies that are susceptible are: *auratum, canadense, cernuum, formosanum, japonicum, rubellum,* and *superbum. L. formosanum* is especially susceptible, and shows up mosaic so quickly that some lily growers scatter plants grown from seed among the lilies in their gardens to act as warning signals.

BOTRYTIS. A third disease, but one that can be curbed with a good spray program, is *botrytis,* a fungus akin to the organism that causes tulip fire. It is most damaging in warm, wet weather; in dry, cool springs it may not be noticeable. It starts as small brownish spots, oval or round, on the foliage, which enlarge often until they merge with each other. Finally the fungus reaches the fruiting stage, which covers the affected parts with a gray mold. Any breeze can then scatter the spores. There is wilting and general collapse of the diseased parts if there is a bad attack. Bulbs are usually not invaded, except those of *L. japonicum,* which are killed. However, the death of parts aboveground is weakening to the bulb. Diseased portions should be removed via a paper bag to minimize scattering the disease.

In gardens where botrytis is a problem, the old mulch can be removed entirely after the plant stalks have been cut away, and replaced with a fresh one after freezing weather.

Garden sanitation is helpful, but a protective spray is also needed. Old-fashioned freshly made Bordeaux mixture is still considered the best control. It must be applied early to be on guard, for it does not cure. All leaf surfaces should be protected, beginning when the plant is a few inches high until the flowers are ready to open. Weekly to ten-day sprays are needed.

The 4-2-50 Bordeaux mixture is made as follows: dissolve five level tablespoons of copper sulphate in a gallon of water in a non-metallic bucket. Mix eight level tablespoons of hydrated lime, bought fresh each season, in two gallons of water in another non-metallic bucket. Pour the copper solution into the lime mixture, stirring constantly. Use a spreader-sticker according to directions on the container. Use immediately. Bordeaux can also be used on peonies for botrytis at the same time, but according to Dr. Cynthia Westcott, is apt to injure tulips when the weather is still cool. Ferbam, a second choice for the lily spray, might be used first to include the tulips, changing to Bordeaux as soon as possible. In airy, sunny gardens it is not necessary in many seasons to spray tulips and peonies.

The madonna lily is especially susceptible to botrytis. If the fall rosette of leaves shows any spots, it should be removed early in spring before the new shoots appear. Other very susceptible kinds are *chalcedonicum, formosanum,* and *testaceum.* Moderately susceptible are *canadense, hansonii, henryi, martagon,* and *superbum.*

APHIDS. These are apt to be the most serious insect pest of lilies in the average garden. Besides carrying viruses, they also may be present in such large numbers that they have a weakening effect. Malathion can be used to control them, but cannot be combined with Bordeaux. When the weather is warm, nicotine sulphate can be added to Bordeaux. It is not effective in cool weather. Aphids cannot be completely controlled with sprays, and in most gardens there are many other plants which harbor aphids. While the new systemic controls may give better results, they are highly poisonous and rapidly absorbed through the skin. They do not seem desirable to use on the home grounds.

Sometimes the growing point of a lily is destroyed, not by disease or insects, but by some mischance. If the remainder of the

The Spanish bluebell flourishes in shady places.

Camassias have starry lavender-blue or white flowers which form spires two or three feet high.

*Allium rosenbachianum album* is one of the tall alliums with flowers forming balls. It is an effective flower for late spring.

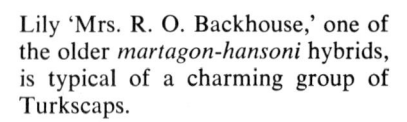

Lily 'Mrs. R. O. Backhouse,' one of the older *martagon-hansoni* hybrids, is typical of a charming group of Turkscaps.

*Above.* The regal lily is typical of the trumpet lily group. Here it graces a midsummer garden in Maine.

*Below.* The pale lilac flowers of *Colchicum autumnale* appear in late August or early September without any foliage.

*Above. Cyclamen neapolitanum* sends up half-inch-long pink or white flowers on 6-inch stems in early autumn. The handsomely marbled leaves come later.

*Below. Crocus longiflorus* blooms at Thanksgiving time with sweet alyssum in a sheltered sunny corner.

plant looks healthy, leave it alone. The following year it will have a chance to recover.

To sum up, lily diseases won't go away if we pretend not to notice them. There are three ways of meeting them. One, plant whatever lilies you like and just keep on planting them. That is expensive and likely to be unsatisfactory. Two, learn which lilies are most resistant to disease and stick to them, with perhaps a minimal spray program. Three, learn a lot about the diseases, strive for the best possible cultural conditions, and be very careful to buy bulbs of superior health reputation, free of mosaic diseases; or learn to grow lilies from seed, as they, too, will be virus-free. A better spray program will go with the last choice, and the person who embarks on this exacting course is on the way to becoming a lily fan.

### CHOOSING LILIES FOR THE GARDEN

CLONES AND STRAINS. It is important to understand the differences between clones and strains in deciding what bulbs to buy.

A *clone* is a group of plants all propagated from the same plant by asexual means—that is, by some form of division of the original plant. Clones of lilies are perpetuated by means of bulbils, bulblets, scales, and by the natural division of a bulb into two or more bulbs. All members of the same clone have the same genes and the same appearance. They share the same susceptibility or resistance to disease, frost damage, and other physiological factors.

The advantage of a clone is the uniformity of all its members. But there is a tremendous disadvantage in the asexual propagation of lilies. If a bulb is infected with a virus, all the bulbs produced by division from it will also be infected.

A *strain* is a group of plants raised from the same parents. It is a very broad term. Some strains contain plants that vary quite widely. Others, when the breeding and selection are carried through several generations, may be quite uniform. A strain may contain in its parentage two or more species, or it may be the result of breeding and selection within one species. When a single plant is selected from a strain and propagated asexually, it and its divisions become a new clone.

A strain can be propagated from seed—and with lilies, this is important, for the viruses of lilies are not transmitted through the seed. Therefore it is possible to produce virus-free bulbs. Because the seed is produced in abundance, it is also possible to offer the bulbs of strains at lower prices than those grown by division.

Many breeders are working for better hybrids and for disease resistance in the species. Bulbs that result from this work cost more and are worth more. There is also a great deal of activity in producing new strains of hybrids and clones of hybrids. Every new generation of seedlings that is raised by an experienced breeder gives the opportunity of selection for more beauty, vigor, and disease resistance. So the gardener who wants lilies should be ever ready to try the newest.

## BEGINNER'S CHOICES

Those just starting out with lilies will find a good range to pick from in the Aurelian hybrids, Mid-Century Hybrids, and Olympic Hybrids. (When the word hybrid is capitalized, it is used as part of a name given to a particular hybrid group by the originator of the group.)

**Aurelian hybrids**

These are a diverse lot developed from *L. henryi,* a species of rugged constitution with strongly reflexed flowers, and several species of Chinese trumpet lilies. They are listed first because they combine vigor and beauty with tolerance to viruses and resistance to basal rot.

Many breeders are producing plants classified as Aurelian

hybrids. Mr. Carleton Yerex coined the term for his own group of offspring of *Lilium aurelianense,* a man-made hybrid of *L. henryi* and *L. sargentiae.* As others raised plants with the same parentage, supplemented with additional closely related species, the term was broadened in its application because of its suitability, so that it now includes a host of strains and clones.

Heights range from 4 to 7 feet. There is a range of flower shapes from trumpet to Turkscap, of color from ivory to deep gold and, more recently, pinks. Bloom is in midsummer. Young shoots are susceptible to frost damage, and should be protected if it threatens.

CARLETON YEREX HYBRIDS

Aurelian Golden Trumpets. One of his early strains varying from yellow to gold.

Flare strains. Autumn Glory Flares, Carnival Flares, etc. Each Flare strain has a dominant color. The flowers are recurved, with strong substance, and bloom later than the trumpet Aurelians, because of the dominance of *L. henryi.*

PALMER-VINELAND HYBRIDS

May be had either as strains or clones. Dr. Slate considers these especially fine because of the splendid flower placement. White, cream, peach, yellow, gold, buff.

DE GRAAFF AURELIAN HYBRIDS

Strains and clones.

Golden Clarion Strain. Trumpet flowers, lemon to gold, 3 to 6 feet. July bloom.

Golden Showers Strain. Flowers pendent, bright yellow inside, brown outside. 4 to 6 feet high. Late July to early August bloom.

Heart's Desire Strain. Bowl-shaped. Soft orange-yellow to cream and white. More subject to virus than other de Graaff Aurelian strains.

Sunburst Strain. Golden yellow, opening into rather starry semi-pendent flowers. 5 to 6 feet. Late July to early August bloom.

**Mid-Century Hybrids** (de Graaff)

This is a variable group derived from the tiger lily (*L. tigrinum*) and several species with upright flowers. Yellow to red, orange, and orange-red flowers which vary in shape from upright bowls to outward-facing and semi-pendent partly reflexed. 2 to 4 feet high in June. They have good resistance to lily troubles.

Mixed hybrids. Include many shapes and colors. Seedlings.

'Enchantment.' Upright cluster of orange-red flaring flowers. 2 to 3 feet. Clone.

'Harmony.' Upright orange flowers on 2- to 3-foot stem. Clone.

'Prosperity.' Lemon-yellow semi-pendent flowers. 3 to 4 feet. Clone.

**Olympic Hybrids** (de Graaff)

A strain of trumpet lilies derived from several Chinese trumpet species. Flowers white, cream, palest pink, or green-tinted inside; greenish-brown to dull rose outside. Fragrant. 3 to 6 feet in midsummer.

## OTHER GARDEN HYBRIDS

The following strains and clones are a selection from the many that are presently offered in this country. They represent only a sample of what is available. Although the complicated array of flowers which plant breeders have brought forth in the last century often obliterates the old classification of lilies by their shapes, they are arranged here more or less according to flower form and the placement of the flowers on the stems. These groups are, roughly, bowl-shaped, upright, reflexed or Turkscap (outward-facing or pendent) and trumpet.

**Auratum hybrids—Bowl-Shaped in Part**

*Lilium auratum* and its varieties, with great bowl-shaped flowers, have been crossed with the trumpets *L. japonicum* and *L. rubellum* and with the Turkscap *L. speciosum*. There are hybrids of all these. There results a diverse group of varied shapes, with colors from white through pink and rose to crimson, rose to crimson spotted, with or without gold or rose bands.

While vigor and disease resistance are improved in some, *L. speciosum* is the only species among the parents that is not dangerously affected by mosaic, so as a group their health must be guarded with care.

Hybrid strains include: Pfeiffer Hybrids, Potomac Hybrids (U.S.D.A.), Centennial Hybrids (Kline); and de Graaff hybrids, named according to color strains. Among the de Graaff strains are Imperial Crimson, Imperial Silver, Imperial Gold, and one called the Jamboree Strain, crimson and white, which Mr. de Graaff considers more disease-resistant.

'Jillian Wallace' is a clone, resulting from an *auratum-speciosum* cross. It is widely distributed in the trade, but the stocks are so likely to be infected with mosaic that it is a risk in the garden if freedom from disease is a goal. There are a number of other named clones.

### Hybrids with Upright Flowers

The low, early-blooming bright orange-red lilies we used to call "umbellatums," and buy in strawberry boxes in the early spring already in bud, all but disappeared during the Second World War, apparently for good, although they are listed by one specialist. They belonged to a hybrid group that has been replaced by new hybrids.

GOLDEN CHALICE HYBRIDS

A de Graaff strain with upright flowers, light yellow to deep yellow, on stems 18 inches to 3 feet in late May. They like full sun and warm locations.

CORONADO HYBRIDS

A de Graaff strain with flowers gold to orange and mahogany red, 2 to 3 feet high, in June.

### Hybrids with Flowers More or Less Reflexed, Outward-Facing or Pendent

*Martagon-hansonii* CROSSES. These lilies have pyramidal spires of small Turkscap flowers, many to a stem, about 5 to 6 feet tall, in early summer. Colors range from pale yellow to orange, lilac, maroon, pink blends and rose, with fine dark maroon spots. *L. martagon* is susceptible to basal rot, but the resistance of *L. hansonii* is imparted to some members of the group. They are not often affected by viruses. They tolerate soils containing lime, and will grow in part shade. The leaves are in whorls. The Pfeiffer Terrace City Hybrids are a strain of this cross. Two clones by Beatrice L. Palmer are 'Ballerina,' chrome yellow dotted maroon, and 'Primadonna,' white dotted pink inside and rose-pink outside.

The older hybrids will probably be entirely superseded by new strains and clones.

BELLINGHAM HYBRIDS

These are based on crosses of several of our West Coast lilies. The reflexed flowers are yellow, orange, and red, strongly spotted. Some flowers are orange-yellow at the heart and orange-red on the outer half of the tepals. The inflorescence is pyramidal, many flowers to a 4- to 6-foot stem in midsummer. As with eastern species, new bulbs are produced from rhizomes. They prefer cool spots and the protection of part shade, but are said to be not long-lived in the East. There are several named clones.

FIESTA HYBRIDS

Strain developed by Dr. N. Abel and de Graaff. Brightly colored reflexed nodding flowers in yellow, red, orange, and maroon, finely dotted with dark maroon. Many flowers on wiry stems 2 to 3½ feet high in midsummer. They prefer full sun, and are said to be virus-resistant.

STENOGRAPHER SERIES

Preston hybrids. Large reflexed outward-facing flowers. Yellow, golden orange, orange-red. Rather susceptible to basal rot.

'Edna Kean.' Deep orange-red flowers. 3 to 4 feet.

'Hurricane.' Cluster of rather flaring flowers that are rather upright. Rich red. 3 to 4 feet.

U.S.D.A. HYBRIDS

*Maximowiczii* Hybrids. Reflexed hybrids facing out and up. Orange-red to red. 3 to 6 feet. Long time of bloom in summer.

PALMER-VINELAND HYBRIDS

'Redbird.' Partly reflexed flowers in a loose pyramid, outward-facing, deep orange-red, finely spotted. Strong stalk to 5 feet tall, in midsummer.

'Algonquin.' Very dark red partly reflexed outward-facing flowers in open pyramid. Flower stalk to 4 feet high in July.

**Trumpet Lilies**

There are notable improvements in the newest trumpet lilies. Not only is there constant selection for vigor, but for greater color range and better flower placement. Many of the trumpet lilies fall into the classification of Aurelian hybrids already discussed.

Green Magic Strain (de Graaff). White, tints of green. 3 to 6 feet. July.

Pink Perfection Strain (de Graaff). Like Olympic Hybrids, but deep pink. Needs cool summers to develop good color.

*Princeps-sulphureum-sulphurgale* Hybrids (Dr. E. F. Palmer). Creamy sulphur. 5 to 7 feet. Midsummer.

Strawberry Hill Strain (Rothman). White, yellow throat; outside flushed rose-purple. 6 feet. July.

Shelburne Hybrids. Pink trumpets.

Temple Strain (John Shaver). Selected strains according to color—pinks to light red, pale greens, white and pearly, and yellow tints. 6 feet. July.

Other breeders in the United States and Canada are producing fine new hybrids. Send for the catalogs of specialists when you see them advertised.

## SPECIES

Here is a group of commonly listed species, varying in their chances for success in the average garden, but fairly well known to many, who would like very much to grow them.

*Lilium auratum,* Goldband Lily. Japan. Large bowl-shaped outward-facing flowers in late July. Flowers fragrant, sometimes a foot across, white, spotted crimson, each tepal banded gold. To 6 feet. There are several color forms. Needs perfect drainage, acid soil. A cool location and shelter from the hottest sun help it to hold its leaves, which are apt to fall prematurely in warm climates. Subject to mosaic and basal rot. A problem plant, though in favored locations, isolated from other lilies, healthy stock may maintain itself very well. Variety *platyphyllum* is a larger and more vigorous plant, but considered by many less graceful.

*L. canadense,* Canada Lily. Eastern North America. Nodding yellow to orange-red bell-shaped flowers in tiers on stems 3 to 5 feet tall in midsummer. Leaves in whorls. New bulb is formed each year at the end of a short rhizome from the old bulb. Grows beside wet ditches and near wet places in meadows, but does well in good moderately acid garden soil, if it stays free of virus and botrytis. Grows naturally in sun, but will tolerate light shade. Graceful and lovely for wild and semi-wild plantings.

*L. candidum,* Madonna Lily. Southeast Europe, southwest Asia. Cherished in gardens for hundreds of years for its short, fragrant white trumpets in June, on stems 4 to 5 feet high. Often fails in gardens after many successful years because of the introduction of basal rot and botrytis. Inferior bulbs often marketed, and their cheap competition prevents successful work on producing better, healthier strains.

Likes sun, withstands drought, tolerates lime. Plant early (August to mid-September) covering only one to two inches. Rosette of leaves should develop in fall, but can be removed in spring before new growth starts to curb spread of botrytis. A joy or a frustration.

*L. formosanum,* Formosa Lily. Fragrant white trumpets, narrow, but tepals flaring at tips, and flushed rose outside, or all white. To 7 feet tall, September. It is susceptible to basal rot, mosaic, and botrytis and is often used as a warning of the presence of mosaic in other bulbs, as spring plants acquire the disease so readily and show the symptoms so well. Easily grown from seed, flowering the same year from winter-sown seed. "Price's Variety" is dwarfer (about 18 inches) with fewer and smaller flowers in midsummer.

*L. henryi.* China. Soft orange Turkscap flowers on stems to 7 feet high in late midsummer. Vigorous, resisting basal rot. Needs protection of high shade during hot part of day to prevent bleaching of flower color. Often needs staking. Susceptible to injury from late spring frosts.

*L. longiflorum,* Easter Lily. Japan. Needs full sun, but mulch well to prevent spring growth from starting too early. Susceptible to virus and botrytis. Plants put out from pots will live in warmer gardens, but this is a risky procedure as far as introducing disease goes. Better to try some of the new tetraploids produced by the U.S. Department of Agriculture. They have larger flowers and heavier substance.

*L. philadelphicum,* Wood Lily. Eastern North America, in thin acid woods and old fields and pastures. Upright orange-scarlet flowers in midsummer on stems to 3 feet high. Charming left where it is, to brighten woods and flaunt its color against the blue of ripening blueberries along gray stone walls. It does not take easily to garden culture.

*L. pumilum* (*tenuifolium*), Coral Lily. East Asia. 18-inch wiry stems carry a small pyramid of little shining scarlet Turkscaps in late spring or early summer. Resists mosaic, but not immune; slightly susceptible to botrytis. Remove seed pods to help lengthen its rather short span of years, but leave one if you want seed, from which it can be grown rather easily, with bloom the second year. Likes full sun. There are yellow forms.

*L. regale,* Regal Lily. China. Large fragrant trumpets, white inside and dull rosy purple outside, on stems 3 to 6 feet high in early July. Sometimes available from local growers dug with a ball of earth when in bud. Improved strains of greater vigor are also available. Less susceptible to viruses than many lilies. Likes sun, increases well.

*L. speciosum.* Japan. Sharply reflexed fragrant flowers, white suffused with rose and spotted deep crimson, horizontal or drooping a little. Bloom in late summer, on stems 3 to 4 feet high.

Resistant to basal rot; somewhat tolerant of viruses, but virus-free bulbs perform better. In warm climates may lose its foliage very early, so profits from cool spot and some shade from hottest sun. New and more vigorous strains and hybrids are likely to replace the species as we now know it. Many are already available.

*L. superbum,* American Turkscap Lily. Eastern North America. Pendent flowers, orange-scarlet spotted with dark maroon, 4 to 7 feet tall, in midsummer. Leaves in whorls. Grows in acid, peaty, but well-drained bog margins and meadows. It is resistant to basal rot, but susceptible to mosaic, and slightly susceptible to botrytis. Lovely in sun or light shade in humusy soil retentive of moisture and rather acid. New bulb formed each year at end of short rhizome produced by old one.

*L. testaceum,* Nankeen Lily. Hybrid between the madonna lily and *L. chalcedonicum,* the scarlet Turkscap lily of Greece. The flowers are reflexed, pale apricot, on stems 4 to 5 feet high, in late June. All stock is said to be infected with mosaic, which it tolerates, but it is a risk to bring into the virus-free garden. Susceptible to basal rot and botrytis.

*L. tigrinum,* Tiger Lily. Asia. Naturalized in New England, and persistent in old gardens there. The semi-pendent orange-red flowers, spotted with deep maroon, are strongly reflexed, and borne on 4- to 6-foot stems in late midsummer. It is easily propagated from the many bulbils. Many stocks are infected with mosaic which is often hard to discern.

## LILIES IN THE GARDEN

The variation in time of bloom and in appearance suggests a great many ways to plant lilies. As long as their basic requirements are met, they may be grown in shrub borders, in perennial borders, in beds by themselves, in light woodlands, and in wild gardens.

If they can be planted so that the plants near them shade the ground and so keep the soil cooler, it is an advantage. The tallest lilies can rise through plants a foot or two high, but the shorter ones can only have quite low plants close around them. If the tall ones rise a good distance above their companion plants, it serves to accentuate their height and dignity. It does not look well for them to appear smothered. There is also the danger of encouraging botrytis if the foliage is crowded so that it cannot get full benefit of air circulation and dry off promptly after rains.

The lower lilies and those with small flowers may be planted in groups of half a dozen or more. If they are to be mixed, there should be limitations to the mixing. A strain that is fairly uniform in size and shape of flowers but has color gradations makes more attractive groupings than a strain where there is variation in shape as well as color. The tallest lilies and those with the largest flowers, such as the sensational new hybrids of *Lilium auratum* with wide-flaring flowers eight or more inches across, should be spaced so that their flowers can be seen effectively, a foot or eighteen inches apart. Just two or three against a green background can make a stunning show without any other bloom near them.

The strong yellow and orange lilies must have companions that harmonize. Blues and lavenders and gray-leaved plants, and of course light yellows and whites, go well with them. Deep violet, too, adds a vigorous note. Where they grow well, delphiniums are superb. The blue *Salvia farinacea* blooms all summer, and is perennial in the Philadelphia area and south. Other flowers for lily time in the blue to violet range are the balloon flower (*Platycodon grandiflorum*) with bell-shaped flowers, the globe thistle (*Echinops*), the veronicas, campanulas, and lavenders. Gray-leaved plants like *Artemisia* 'Silver Mound' and 'Silver King' are effective foils to highly colored lilies.

Other good companion plants are Paris daisies or marguerites, usually obtainable as small plants in two- or three-inch pots. They can be set in between earlier-flowering bulbs such as tulips and daffodils, and will grow into bushy plants a foot or so wide and almost as high. The pale yellow form is more effective than the white one, and is more vigorous. They are tender perennials, and in cold climates must be set out anew each spring.

In many an old garden, orange-red tiger lilies bloom with magenta phlox, a most unhappy combination. But with white phlox, blue salvia and globe thistle, and some soft yellows, tigers are a handsome sight.

A strain like the Bellingham Hybrids or Fiesta Hybrids which contains within itself a wide range of color is displayed to better advantage if it is interplanted with only one or two other kinds of plants. It might rise from a ground cover of periwinkle (*Vinca minor*), or lavender, or a fern such as New York fern, which will endure sun, but still does not grow too rampant.

Lilies with softer and paler colors, the Aurelians, Olympics, madonnas, and other whites, can of course be planted with a wide range of gay summer plants—the good, clear-colored phloxes, bee-balms in pink and red-purple, with flowers in the blue to violet range, and light yellows. Madonna lilies and delphiniums are a well-known combination. Regal lilies and delphiniums are another fine pair with a little more animation which comes from less rigid stems and the brushing of rosy brown on the outside of the tepals of the lilies.

There are many annuals that are in bloom at lily time. Personal taste will devise ways of using them. The lilies, however, for health and beauty, should be allowed to dominate any group of which they are a part. The harshness of too many zinnias and marigolds would detract from them.

Roses, especially the lower floribundas, make an excellent foil for lilies, but it should be remembered that roses harbor many aphids, and a regular rose spray program should be followed to control those disease carriers.

All in all, the outward-facing and pendent lilies, especially the taller ones, are the most dramatic flowers of the summer garden. Their qualities should be displayed to advantage, not lost in mere masses of color supplied by other flowers. Even one fine stalk should be so placed that it catches and holds the eye.

CHAPTER IX

# Late Summer and Autumn Bulbs

It is true that the lilies are the queens of summer, but there are other very attractive hardy summer bulbs that deserve notice, too. There are some with lily-like flowers that are well suited to the late garden. Others, such as the *fall-flowering crocuses* and *colchicums,* may seem out of season to those who have never grown them. They are in full bloom at the very time we are finishing up our autumn gardening tasks and planting their relatives for spring bloom. They appear like little prophets, foretelling the joys of spring. They make the winter seem shorter, for there are not many weeks between the last crocus of fall and the first crocus of spring.

## AMARCRINUM

*Amarcrinum howardii* (*Crinodonna corsii*). A hybrid species between *Amaryllis belladonna* and *Crinum moorei.* It has soft pink rather fragrant flowers like trumpet lilies on stems up to 4 feet high in late summer and early autumn. The foliage, which persists through the year, is strap-shaped. It is not hardy where there is prolonged freezing weather, but in mild areas it grows into large clumps and is valued for its long blooming period. Technically, the name *Crinodonna* has precedence over the name *Amarcrinum*. The cross was made both in Europe and in California, but the European one was made first, and was named *Crinodonna*. But the plants grown in the United States, the results of the American cross, are commonly called *Amarcrinum*. Apparently the plants of both crosses look alike.

## COLCHICUMS

Although colchicums are not related to crocuses, and even belong to a different family (the Lily Family), they resemble them so much that they are commonly called "autumn crocus." They differ from crocuses in several important ways. The corms are large, about two to four inches long, and are poisonous. Corms and foliage are immune to rodent damage. The foliage, produced in spring, is also large, sometimes nearly 2 feet high, with leaves up to four inches wide. While the new crocus corm forms on top of the old one, the colchicum corm grows beside the old one. There is also another important difference. They cost more. But they are permanent, increasing into large clumps which produce a succession of many flowers for several weeks in early fall.

There are some sixty species of *Colchicum,* distributed through Europe, the Mediterranean area, and temperate Asia. The ones commonly grown are fall-blooming and rosy lilac or white. The poisonous element, colchicine, has long been used in the treatment of gout. Recently it has been used in plant breeding to create tetraploid plants by inducing doubling of the chromosome number.

Although there is some variation in the size and coloring of the commonly grown colchicums, their general effect in the garden is pinkish lilac or white. Some are tessellated or checkered when the flowers first open, but the checks fade in two or three days.

Colchicum flowers are taller than those of crocuses, rising from 6 to 10 inches aboveground. The long perianth tube is partly underground, like that of the crocus. The colored part of the flower is usually two to three inches long. The flowers start to emerge in late summer, usually after a good rain. Bloom may be had for a period of about six weeks. Planting should be done as soon as the corms are procurable, usually late August or early September. If they bloom before they are planted, it does not damage the bulbs. Place them eight to ten inches apart, and cover with about three or four inches of soil.

*Colchicum autumnale.* This is the species most commonly offered. It is soft pink-lilac, and starts to bloom in early September. Its variety *album,* slightly smaller and not pure white, is useful, though less attractive than *C. speciosum album.*

*C. byzantinum.* This is the earliest to bloom here, sometimes beginning in late August. It has light tessellations. It is vigorous, with very large, broad leaves and many rosy-lilac flowers.

*C. speciosum.* The flowers of this fine species are larger, the substance better, and the color stronger than those of *C. autumnale.* Its pure white variety is beautifully shaped and very choice. With us, these two start to bloom toward the end of September. The variety *bornmuelleri* starts to bloom almost a month earlier.

There are many named garden forms and hybrids. The following all start to flower in early September, and have some tessellations on first opening: 'Guizot,' large, bright rosy lilac; 'Premier,' paler, with large flowers; 'Princess Astrid,' large, with the brightest color; 'Lilac Wonder,' narrow tepals that open out flat.

In our garden, two or three double varieties have not had the vigor of the single, but they are very pretty, in lilac or white.

FOLIAGE CONSIDERATIONS. Attractive though the colchicums are, their foliage is an undeniable problem. The large masses of leaves appear very early in spring, and are presentable at first. They quickly grow to their full size. During May they start to flop over, and during June turn yellow and finally brown and withered. They should not be removed until they pull away easily. So the bulbs must be planted where the fall flowers can be admired, but where the leaves will not detract from the spring picture, and perhaps actually damage nearby plants during the ripening period.

We have them in several locations. There are groups in pachysandra, and the flowers show well above it. Many are planted in ferns, which do very well at concealing the aging leaves, but are a little too high for a good view of the flowers. The ferns could be cut down in mid-August, and would just be coming up again as the flowers appeared, but this is a nuisance. Perhaps the best spot is at the edge of a woodland planting of rhododendrons. Here flowers by the hundred are a wonderful sight in September, and the browning foliage mingles unobtrusively with the natural layer of old tree leaves on the ground in June.

It is best to try just a dozen or so corms at first. Since one produces a great many flowers, a group of three or four makes a good spot of color. Just a few groups will add interest to the edge of a shrub border or to the planting near a front door. A few will add interest to a patch of periwinkle or pachysandra.

## AUTUMN CROCUS

Of the many species of *Crocus* that bloom in the fall and on into winter, we can list only a few. These true crocuses are as delightful as the spring ones, and just as attractive to rodents. The foliage is small and grassy, and no problem at all in appearance. But like other winter-green foliage, it needs sun and protection from the sweep of wind. Like colchicums, autumn-flowering crocuses should be planted at the earliest possible moment in late summer or fall, spaced two to four inches apart, and covered two inches.

*Crocus speciosus.* If just one autumnal kind is to be planted, this should be the one. It is lovely, hardy, and vigorous, following the colchicums into bloom in early October. It is a good blue-violet, and has a very fine white form. A number of named varieties may be had, but in a small collection they do not seem enough different from the species to be worth seeking.

*C. kotschyanus* (long known and usually listed as *C. zonatus*). This is easy to come by. It is a good grower and increaser, with light lilac flowers that appear in early October.

*C. laevigatus.* A small flower of pale lilac feathered darker outside. This and its variety *fontenayi,* with more prominent feathering, bloom in November, and may send up flowers even later when the weather is favorable.

*C. longiflorus.* The lilac flowers appear in November. I had it for several years in the sheltered corner of a rock garden where it came up through a blanket of sweet alyssum at Thanksgiving time. Then the squirrels found it.

This is but a meager sample of a delightful tribe. Some supposedly rather tender ones do well in a sunny, protected spot, so it is worth trying any you happen to see in your local garden mart. The blooming times are rather erratic, perhaps because of local moisture conditions.

Ten or a dozen of a kind make a fine group, and a planting of several kinds, the colored ones alternating with white ones, are charming set off only by crisp newly fallen autumn leaves. But do not let the leaves cover them. I have always wanted to make a planting of the handsome late October-flowering *Cimicifuga simplex,* with its graceful spires of white flowers and lacy foliage rising from a bed of blue-violet *Crocus speciosus,* but never had a suitable rodent-free site to try it. It would be a feature in the shady corner of a small city back yard.

## CYCLAMEN

The flowers of the hardy cyclamens are miniature versions of the florists' cyclamen, well known as a pot plant, with the same back-swept petals, but a narrower range of color patterns.

They must be considered difficult, but far from impossible to grow.

The genus *Cyclamen* contains about twelve species and some wild forms and varieties, belonging to the Primrose Family, and found in the Mediterranean region and central Europe. The storage portion of the plant looks like a corm, but is a tuber that grows larger each year, quite able, it is said, to reach the size of a dinner plate, and producing more flowers yearly.

Because of the expansion of the tubers, it is well to plant them about ten inches apart. It is hard to tell the upper sides of tubers that have been dried, and remnants of roots must be looked for very carefully. *C. neapolitanum* produces most of its roots from the top and sides, few from the bottom. The top is slightly hollowed, the bottom rounded. *C. coum* and *C. europaeum* root at the bottom.

Some growers in the Pacific Northwest supply newly dug tubers with roots intact. Top and bottom are clearly evident, and the fresh condition of the plants makes success with them far more likely.

Picking the site for cyclamens is half the success in growing them. They should have protection from hot sun and also from cold winter winds, which are apt to destroy the handsome foliage by drying the slender leaf stalks. The soil should be well drained and amply supplied with humus. A good top dressing of leaf mold in late summer helps to protect the foliage. Although it is often suggested that cyclamens need lime, we have had them growing for six years in the shelter of hemlocks and rhododendrons in soil that is undoubtedly acid. They have been better each year, and the foliage has weathered a bitter winter with no snow cover.

*Cyclamen neapolitanum.* This is the one to try first, for it is the most dependable of the hardy cyclamens. It is also a little beauty. The pink flowers, on scapes 4 to 5 inches high, appear during the late summer and fall. The leaves, rather variable, emerge at the same time, shaped like elongated hearts, or sometimes like ivy leaves. They are green marbled with silver and darker green. The following summer they die away. There is a lovely white-flowered form, *album*.

*C. europaeum.* The deep rose, fragrant flowers appear in August. There is also a white form. The leaves are present most of the year, roundly heart-shaped, with rather indistinct marbling.

*C. coum.* The flowering time of this chubby little flower varies with climate. In England and the mid-South it blooms from January to March, but near Philadelphia it holds back until March. Through the late fall and winter it can be enjoyed by those who like very small things, for the buds lie with crimson cheeks against the ground all that time. The rounded leaves have no marbling, and the undersides are dull rose.

## LYCORIS

A small genus of bulbous plants of the Amaryllis Family, native to the temperate parts of China and Japan.

*L. radiata,* Spider-Lily. (Often wrongly called *Nerine sarniensis,* a name belonging to an entirely different and more tender plant.) This is on the borderline of hardiness in the Philadelphia region, but can be grown in sheltered places where its leaves, green all winter, get some protection. Bright coral-red flowers appear before the foliage in September, on scapes about a foot high. Their narrow, sharply recurved tepals and long stamens suggest the common name. In climates milder than that of Philadelphia, it forms fine clumps; in harsher climates, increase is slower and more uncertain.

*L. squamigera* (*Amaryllis halli*). Sometimes called hardy amaryllis. This is much hardier than the spider-lily, successful as far north as Albany and Boston. The foliage, which resembles that of a vigorous trumpet daffodil, appears in early spring and dies away in June. In August, the scapes shoot up rapidly to a height of 3 or more feet, each bearing at its summit several fragrant lilac-pink lily-like flowers about three inches long.

They can be planted near shrubs, or in thin woodland, or in the flower garden. The long naked scapes need low vegetation about them. Ferns are excellent, or low annuals of colors that will enhance, not kill, the delicate tints of the flowers. Petunias in deep violet, lavender, white, or rose, or snapdragons or verbenas look well. Orange and strong yellows should be avoided.

Clumps should be divided when they become very thick. They can be lifted in June, dried for about a month, and replanted. Plant eight to ten inches apart to allow for increase. Cover with about four inches of soil.

## STERNBERGIA LUTEA

Often this plant is called yellow fall crocus, and the flowers do look like crocuses. It belongs to a small Old World genus of the Amaryllis Family. Flowers and leaves appear during the autumn, the flowers a rich golden yellow standing about 6 inches high. The leaves need winter sun and protection from cold winds. In the Philadelphia area and north, although they are hardy, persisting and thriving for years, bloom is not always as plentiful as the amount of foliage seems to indicate it should be. To the south, the bulbs increase fast enough to need division every few years. In the North, they can be left alone much longer

Sternbergias can be planted in grass where the sod is not too thick, and look well under deciduous trees. Or they can be clumped any place where there is some winter sun and shelter, even though it is shaded in summer. Plant about six inches apart to give room to the leaves, and cover with three inches of soil.

CHAPTER X

# Bulbs to Bloom Indoors

The hardy bulbs that bloom in the first part of spring can be persuaded to advance their flowering time so that they can be enjoyed indoors during the winter. A pot of white daffodils or of golden crocuses or blue hyacinths adds wonderful cheer to a room. A beautiful snow scene outside the window can be enjoyed all the more when there is a bright promise of spring inside.

A few of the forcing bulbs listed here are not among the hardiest, but are included because they are among the easiest to force successfully. For the hardiest, it is necessary to simulate the conditions under which they thrive outside, while shortening the time they ordinarily need to come into bloom by giving them warmth sooner than they would have it naturally.

THE CONDITIONS FOR GOOD FLOWERS. Successful bloom from hardy bulbs is based on the following stages of growth: *First,* the rooting period, lasting six to twelve weeks, with the temperature about 40° to 45° and without light. *Second,* an intermediate period during which the plants are given more warmth (about 50° to 55°) and light but no direct sunlight. This encourages slow top growth, and lasts from ten days to three weeks. *Third,* the plants are moved into as much light and sun as possible until the buds start to open. *Fourth,* at the start of flowering, they should be given a spot out of direct sun. If possible, these last two places should be below 70°, so that the flowers will stay in good condition for a long time. Moving them to a cool place at night is also beneficial, especially if daytime temperatures go above 70°.

Before growing bulbs in pots, it may be well to try some in pebbles and water to check on the growing conditions in your house. If they grow long limp leaves, and the flower buds turn brown without opening, or the flowers dry up as fast as they open, your house may well be too hot and dry. A lower setting of the thermostat, careful ventilation if temperatures go unexpectedly high, and increased humidity are needed. Unless you are able to make these modifications, it is better to grow other house plants.

## FORCING BULBS IN WATER

Easiest of all bulbs to force is the airy "Paper White," *Narcissus tazetta papyraceus*. Success begins—as it must in bringing all these bulbs into flower in the house—with good bulbs, and large ones. Continuous bloom may be had by starting bulbs at two-week intervals from the end of October until early February. The ones started in October should bloom for Christmas.

Choose a container that has room for a large mass of roots. An all-over average depth of close to four inches is the minimum. If you have any horticultural charcoal, put a piece or two in the bottom of the container, then fill it to within an inch of the top with pebbles. Set the bulbs close together but not touching, and press them about half an inch into the pebbles. Add water so that it reaches the surface of the pebbles. Then take the bowl to a cool, airy, and darkened place. Complete darkness is not needed. A cool cellar is excellent. I use our garage, which is heated but not hot, setting the bowls on an open shelf away from the window (which can be opened as needed) where the light is dim.

I keep bulbs waiting for later planting here, too, in open

shallow baskets, for they must be kept cool to preserve their vitality, but must not freeze.

Be sure that there is always water touching the base of the bulb until the roots have started. Then keep it just below the bulb base. When there is a good mass of roots and the top growth is up an inch or so, move the bulbs to a lighter place. Ours are moved in front of the garage window, which faces north. Some people use cellar windows. After a week, they can be moved into the house and given as much light as possible, including sun. As the plants grow, they use more water, so be sure the level is kept up. Sunlight keeps the plants from growing tall and ungainly, but as soon as the buds start to open, it is best to move them out of direct sun for a longer flowering period.

If bulbs that have been forced in water are naturally hardy in the area, they can be planted outside successfully afterward. But that must wait for mild weather. Until spring comes, they must be given light and water. Finally they can be taken out and slipped into the ground just as they come from the bowl, with any pebbles that do not shake easily out of the matted roots. They should be planted in some out-of-the-way place where they can recover slowly and start to bloom again.

Other kinds that can be grown in water are the yellow and orange counterpart of the "Paper White"—'Grand Soleil d'Or' or, more simply, "Soleil d'Or," and poetaz varieties. The poetaz should not be started until mid-November, and need a good cool month for root development. Roman hyacinths can also be forced in pebbles, after two cool months for rooting. Hyacinths in glasses are discussed under forcing hyacinths (*see* page 173).

## FORCING BULBS IN SOIL

Aside from the necessity of starting with the best bulbs, the ability to control temperatures during the growing period is most vital for good forcing. For the essential period of cold and dark, pots can be buried outdoors. It is also possible, with proper attention, to use attics, cellars, and garages. Fluctuations of heat and cold must be controlled as much as possible, for those fluctuations out of control can cancel out all effort. Alternate freezing and thawing are especially harmful. An open attic is a risky place, and if bulbs are to be rooted there, they should be heavily protected. An unused but plastered room where heat can be turned off and outside air given if needed is excellent. Have a thermometer handy for frequent checking. A high-low thermometer, which gives a record of highs and lows, is a good garden tool which is useful in forcing.

Most modern cellars are hot and dry, but a window can often be arranged to give the right temperature in a cellar room, or a section can be closed off around a window to give a place for starting bulbs.

Clay pots called bulb pans are usually used for bulbs. These are wider than they are high. Attractive glazed containers with drainage holes can also be used. Forced bulbs look better in containers that are broader than tall. Pans can vary from six inches to twelve inches across, depending on the number of bulbs to be planted. If old pans are used, they should be scrubbed inside and out. Clay containers should be soaked overnight before they are used.

A potting medium may be mixed as follows: 2 parts of topsoil, 1 part of compost, leaf mold, or peat moss, and up to 1 part of sand or vermiculite. Vermiculite is light, and easy to use and store. If the topsoil is quite sandy, no sand or vermiculite will be needed, but if it is very heavy, use the full amount.

Perfectionists will shake the mixture through a soil sieve. Those who have no sieve can break up lumps and pick out sticks and stones. Although it is not necessary to add fertilizer, since the bulbs will bloom well without it, if the bulbs are to go outside after forcing, a complete fertilizer such as 4-12-8 or 5-10-10 can be mixed in. About a tablespoon to two quarts of soil is enough. It is also possible to use some of the fertilizers packaged for use on house plants when the pans are brought into the light instead of mixing it in the soil at the start. But better too little than too much fertilizer for bulbs.

The finished planting mixture should be moist, but not wet. Place a piece of broken pot or a rough stone over the hole in the pan, and add a few more pieces of pot or stone around it. Over them put an inch-thick layer of peat moss, coarse leaf mold, or the material that was too large to go through the sieve. Add a layer of potting soil to the level that would bring the bulbs placed on it to ½ inch from the top of the pan. Press the bulbs into this layer gently, spaced ½ inch to an inch apart. Fill in around them with more soil, and press it in with the fingers so that it is firm but not packed. Cover with a thin layer of soil that just hides the bulbs. Stand the finished pan in a dish of water until the top surface is well moistened. Remove the dish and let the excess water in the pan drain away. Label it with the name of the bulb and the planting date.

If the pan is to spend the cold period indoors, it can be slipped into a polyethylene bag and closed at the top with an elastic. Although I have not used the bags outdoors, I see no reason why they could not be put there, too. They would keep out worms and slugs, and would be a safeguard against both flooding and drying out.

If the pans are to be kept inside, they do not need to be all potted up at the same time, but if they are to be buried outside, it is easier to do the whole job and be done with it. Bulbs not planted must of course be kept in a cool, airy spot, and planting should take place within two or three weeks if they are to flower before spring.

Indoor fluctuations of temperature can be eased by putting the pans in crates and stuffing newspapers in around them. If mice are a possibility, invert pans of the same size over them. All can be covered with sacks, old blankets, or other insulating material.

If the bulbs are to spend the rooting period outdoors, pick a site that is well drained and shaded at least in part. Here again the object is to maintain an even temperature. The trench should be deep enough for a layer of drainage material, the pots or pans, and a layer of protective material on top to prevent solid freezing so that the bulbs can be removed easily during the winter. Plan the order in which bulbs are to be removed, and make a chart of their location.

Unless the trench will drain quickly and perfectly, put a layer of gravel or small stones in the bottom, and set the pots on it. Pack leaves or peat moss in around the pots. All bulbs but daffodils need rodent protection: either inverted pots or squares of hardware cloth bent down around the rims. A good layer of leaves, straw, or salt hay goes over all and well beyond the trench on all sides, held in place by wire or branches.

It is best to sink the bulbs on a cool day when soils have cooled. Put on part of the top cover, and wait for the final layer until the first cold weather. A thick mulch of about eighteen inches will insulate against mild as well as cold spells once the ground is cool.

BRINGING THE BULBS INTO BLOOM. The pans should be checked at intervals of a month to be sure that they are moist enough. Once a bulb has started to make its roots, drying out can be serious and damage the flower buds. At the end of the second month, examine some of the pots from which you expect the first bloom, to see if roots are showing at the drainage holes and around the edges at the surface of the soil. If so, a few can be brought into the place they are to occupy during the next stage of their development. If they must be brought in from outdoors, pick a time when the air is above freezing.

In this next stage, with light but no sun and a temperature as near 50° to 55° as possible, the plants will stay from ten days to three weeks. They will begin to need water more frequently now, especially if they are not in polyethylene bags. As those in bags make top growth, the bags must be opened and rolled down a little every day or so to accustom the plant slowly to drier air.

When a few inches of top growth has been made and the flower buds show, move the plants into as much light and sun as possible. Remove the bags. The plants will need more water. They will probably be in a warmer temperature, but preferably below 70°. When the flowers start to open, move them out of the sun. During the last two stages of growth and flowering, the bloom will last longer if the pans are moved to a cooler place at night.

CARE AFTER THE BLOOMING PERIOD. Bulbs to be saved for planting outside need water and light for the rest of their growing period. When the foliage starts to yellow, give less water, finally letting the pan dry in some out-of-the-way corner. Bulbs forced later will still be green when spring comes, but wait until the weather is mild before planting them. Slip them out of the pot and plant them in a group. Bulbs that have dried off can be separated when they are planted. It may take two or three years for forced bulbs to bloom again, but often they bloom the next year.

Forced bulbs from the florist should have the same care given to home-grown bulbs, and they, too, can be planted outside.

## PRECOOLED AND SPECIALLY PREPARED BULBS

Hyacinths intended for forcing are given a special temperature treatment in the Netherlands which shortens the period necessary to bring them into bloom by about three weeks. The treatment has a permanent effect on the bulbs, and even those potted after Christmas will bloom much more quickly than untreated bulbs. Daffodils and tulips meant for forcing are often available from dealers who have had them precooled in this country, and as soon as they are delivered, you must be prepared to pot them promptly, as the effects of the treatment soon wear off unpotted bulbs.

A friend of mine who has an extra refrigerator to devote to plant use does her own precooling. She uses bulbs from her garden as well as those she buys. The refrigerator is set for 40°, and the bulbs are precooled for a minimum of six weeks, but some are kept in it for two or three months before they are potted up. Every two weeks she takes some out, pots them, and puts them under a bench in her little garden room where it is dark and cool. She uses the refrigerator to start hyacinths in glasses, keeping them in the cold until the glasses are well filled with roots. Daffodils, crocuses, grape-hyacinths, early scillas, and *Iris reticulata* are all satisfactorily handled this way, but tulips have been less successful.

A few little bulbs like crocuses and scillas could easily be tucked away in the back of a family refrigerator, which should be set at the lowest temperature compatible with proper food storage.

## FORCING HYACINTHS

Specially prepared hyacinths are very satisfactory to grow in soil. A six-inch pan of just three bulbs is a very pretty sight and easy to handle, and there is a time advantage in having three or four small pots instead of one or two large ones. Three hyacinths in a room at one time are enough for most people, because of the heavy perfume. It takes about fifteen weeks to bring treated hyacinths into bloom, and those potted in early September should bloom in time for Christmas.

The attractive new hyacinth glasses now available should make many people want to try them. First drop a piece of charcoal into the glass, then fill it with water to the point where the glass widens out. When the bulb, which should be top size, is placed in the glass, it should just touch the water. Keep the glass in a cool, dark place until the roots have well filled it, and the top is up about two inches. The water level must be maintained at the bottom of the bulb until the roots start to grow, and then kept just a shade below it.

After the hyacinth is brought out into the light, tie around the glass a piece of thin cardboard which extends above it for about a foot. Narrow it at the top so that it forms a cone with an opening about four inches across. The stalk of the flower will lengthen as it reaches up to the light. Similar cones should be made for potted hyacinths. Take them off when the stalk has lengthened enough to hold the flowers above the leaves.

The starred varieties of hyacinths in the list in Chapter IV are good for forcing. In addition, there are a few called multiflora or fairy hyacinths. Instead of having one large spike, each bulb produces several slender spires hung with ten or twenty bells. Since the spires do not all develop at the same time, there is a long season of bloom. These pretty hyacinths may not be specially prepared. Ask whether they have been when you buy them, so that you will know what to expect of them.

## DAFFODILS

Two good daffodil varieties to try are 'Carlton,' the splendid yellow large cup, and 'Mount Hood,' a vigorous white trumpet. They are always welcome afterward in the garden. Varieties that are available precooled can be counted on as being good for forcing.

The following are considered among the best:

YELLOW TRUMPETS. Golden Harvest, Rembrandt, Unsurpassable.

BICOLOR TRUMPETS. Music Hall, Spring Glory.

WHITE TRUMPETS. Beersheba, Mount Hood, Mrs. Ernst H. Krelage.

LARGE CUPS. Scarlet Elegance, Dunkeld, Rustom Pasha—yellow with red; Brunswick—yellow cup; Flower Record—orange cup; Mrs. R. O. Backhouse—apricot-pink cup.

SMALL CUPS. La Riante, Verger—white with bright cups.

DOUBLE. Irene Copeland—white with yellow; Twink—yellow with red.

TRIANDRUS. Thalia.

CYCLAMINEUS. February Gold, Peeping Tom—yellow.
JONQUILLA. Trevithian—yellow.
POETAZ. Cragford, Geranium—white and red; Scarlet Gem—yellow and red.
POETICUS. Actaea.

However, any daffodils except the late ones will rush the season if they have three or more months of cold outdoors and are not forced too early. The earliest to bloom out of doors should be brought in first. Some of the shorter and smaller daffodils are delightful in the house, for example, 'Bambi,' 'W. P. Milner,' and the tiny *Narcissus asturiensis* (*minimus*).

## TULIPS

These are more difficult for good home forcing. They must be brought along slowly, and it is probably difficult for most people to give them the proper temperatures while their tops are developing. Crocuses, too, must not be forced fast. For your first attempt at tulips, try some early doubles. The flowers are large and showy enough to give an effect even if some bulbs in the pan do not bloom.

When planting tulips, place the outside circle of bulbs with their flat sides against the pot. When they are brought into the second stage of growth, they should have ten days to two weeks in dim light to lengthen the flower stems, then be given full light.

There are many good forcing tulips. If you are successful with the early doubles, check with your dealer to see what forcing varieties he will have in the fall, preferably precooled, so that you can order them ahead.

## SMALL BULBS

All kinds of crocuses, small scillas, grape-hyacinths, the spring starflower (*Ipheion*), and small bulbous iris can be flowered indoors. Snowdrops and crocuses fade quickly in warm rooms, and unless cool spots can be found for them, there seems to be little use in trying them.

There is a pleasant satisfaction in having a few pots of bulbs to fuss over during the time that outdoor gardening is suspended. Watching the growth of the roots, the sprouting of the leaves, the emergence of the buds, and their final unfolding is a day-to-day diversion. When spring comes, we are apt to be too busy to observe these miniature but marvelous pageants of nature. A dozen "Paper Whites" and a half dozen each of hyacinths and daffodils will be a good introduction to the pleasures of growing hardy bulbs indoors.

# Glossary

ASEXUAL REPRODUCTION. Reproduction of a plant by some means other than by seeds. Grafting, cuttings ("slips"), and division of the root system are among the methods used.
AXIL. The upper angle of a leaf and the stem on which it is borne at the point of juncture.
BLASTING. The withering or decay of a flower bud.
BLIND. Not producing an expected flower.
BULB. A modified bud, usually underground, consisting of a short stem and a number of short, fleshy leaves or portions of leaves.
BULBEL, BULBIL, BULBLET. A small immature bulb. Some regard the three words as synonymous. Others call the bulbs that form above ground bulbels or bulbils, and the bulbs that form underground bulblets.
CALYX. See SEPAL.
CHROMOSOME. A unit of heredity in the nucleus of a cell. Chromosomes usually occur in pairs which are similar or identical to each other in appearance. There may be one to over a hundred to a nucleus. Each species has its own number and kinds of chromosomes. In plants, every cell contains this proper number except certain cells which are formed during the reproductive process which contain half the number, one from each pair. A cell unites with a reproductive cell of the opposite sex, which also contains half the characteristic number, and the resulting new cell contains the normal number of chromosomes, which form new pairs, containing hereditary factors from both parent cells.
CLONE. All the descendants of a single plant, produced from it asexually, usually by division of the root stock, by runners, cuttings, or grafting. Well-known examples of clones are the 'Delicious' apple, the 'Peace' rose, and the 'Red Emperor' tulip. Since all the plants produced asexually have identical chromo-

somes, they are all like each other and all like the parent plant. However, deviations sometimes occur through sporting. The seedlings of a clone which are the result of the sexual process are not members of the clone, and not entitled to the clonal name, no matter how much they may resemble it. A seedling may be selected, propagated asexually, and therefore become a new clone with a new name.

COLOR. In this book, certain names of colors which are often used rather loosely are used precisely. Crimson is red with a little blue in it. Scarlet is bright red with a little yellow in it. Violet is midway between blue and red. Purple is violet with a little red in it. Lilac is pale violet with a little pink in it. Lavender is violet with blue in it.

CORM. A short swollen stem containing stored food and bearing buds or growing shoots on its surface.

CORMEL. A small corm arising from a mother corm.

COROLLA. See PETAL.

CORONA. An appendage of a flower (especially typical of daffodils) immediately surrounding the stamens and pistils in the center of the flower. In the daffodil, a long corona is called a trumpet; one of medium size is called a crown or cup, and a very small one is called an eye. There is no definite borderline between one term and another.

CROSS (noun). The offspring of two plants of the same species (see HYBRID).

CROWN. The words "crown" and "cup" are often used interchangeably in speaking of daffodils with coronas shorter than the length of the perianth segments. I have tried to use the word "crown" for those coronas which are shorter than the perianth segments, and either very flat, or very frilled and scalloped. The word "cup" is used for coronas which are actually cup-shaped.

CULTIVAR. A plant variety that has originated in cultivation, as distinct from one that has developed in the wild without man's intervention. A wild variety is generally self-perpetuating; a cultivar is most frequently propagated by vegetative means, or asexually.

CUP. See CROWN.

EYE. In daffodils, the corona when it is very short, as in the poet's narcissus.

FAMILY. A group of genera which have in common certain characters of flower and fruit which show them to be closely related. A few families contain but one genus each; some many hundreds. A *genus* (plural, *genera*) consists of a group of species the flower and fruit structures of which show them to be even more closely related than those in a family. It is possible to hybridize many of the species in the same genus, even though they do not ordinarily hybridize in the wild because of geographical isolation from each other, or different blooming seasons, or some other reason. A genus may contain from one to hundreds of species. The name of one of the genera in a family is used in modified form for the family name. The genus *Iris* belongs to the Iris Family or *Iridaceae*, which also contains the genera *Crocus, Gladiolus, Freesia,* and others; the genus *Ranunculus* (buttercup) belongs to the Buttercup Family or *Ranunculaceae*, which contains also *Anemone, Eranthis* (winter-aconite), and such seemingly different plants as *Clematis, Delphinium,* and *Aquilegia.*

A *species* is a group of individuals which bear a strong resemblance to each other, and which commonly breed among themselves to produce offspring like themselves. The members of the same species have the same genetic make-up, although minor variations occur from time to time.

A *variety* is a plant which varies from others of its species in a minor characteristic. White flowers, for example, often occur in a species with colored flowers. There are also varieties of garden origin, and to these the recently coined word "cultivar" is often applied.

Studies of plants often result in revision of their status. Species may be moved from one genus to another, or reduced from species to subspecies, and so forth. Botanists also differ in their concepts of what constitutes a certain grouping, some recognizing more genera, species, or varieties than others.

GENE. Part of a chromosome, a hereditary factor.

GENUS. See under FAMILY.

HEELING-IN. A form of temporary planting. Plants are usually heeled-in by placing them close together in a trench, perhaps at an angle instead of upright, and covering the underground parts with soil.

HUMUS. Partially decomposed organic matter, animal or vegetable or both, in or on the soil. It is usually dark in color.

HYBRID. A hybrid is the offspring obtained by the crossing of two species. The offspring obtained from crosses within a species are called "crosses." Sometimes, however, they come to be called "hybrids," too, as with French hybrid lilacs, which are supposed to be the result of crossing and selection within a single species.

INFLORESCENCE. A flowering shoot; usually applied to a shoot with more than one flower.

MULCH. A protective layer on the surface of the soil. It may consist of ground corn cobs, sawdust, pine needles, straw, salt hay, buckwheat hulls, leaves, compost, gravel or small stones, or other material. The topmost layer of the soil itself, cultivated and pulverized, is called a dust mulch. The mulch serves to maintain soil temperatures at as constant a level as possible, to conserve soil moisture, to retard weed growth, to keep fruit or flowers clean. It should admit water from above freely, but retard evaporation from the soil surface.

NODE. The joint-like point on a stem where one or more leaves appear; if covered with soil, roots are apt to grow at the node instead of leaves.

OFFSET. A plant originating from a mother plant, usually from a short side shoot.

PERIANTH. The part of a flower that encloses the pistils and stamens; in garden flowers, usually the brightly colored part that makes the plant attractive for ornamental use. In many bulbous plants, the perianth consists of six segments which look alike or almost alike. These segments are often called "tepals."

PETAL. The perianth is often composed of two parts. The inner one, or *corolla,* may be divided into separate units called "petals," as in the rose, or only partly divided into petals, as in the cyclamen, or not divided at all, as in the morning-glory, or otherwise modified. The outer part of the perianth is the *calyx,* composed of sepals (see SEPAL).

ROGUE. A nontypical or inferior plant. Roguing is the process of removing plants not true to name, diseased, or having some unwanted trait.

SCAPE. A leafless flower stalk.

SEPAL. A unit of the calyx, the outer part of the perianth when it is in two parts. The sepals may be united into one piece, or separate. They may be green and inconspicuous, or they may be the brightly colored part of the flower, as in anemones and winter-aconites.

SPECIES. See under FAMILY.

SPORT. A change in the tissues of a plant producing a variation from the normal appearance. Many new cultivars arise from sports. They may differ in color, in form, or in some other characteristic. Sometimes sports turn out to be unstable, with a tendency to revert to the appearance of the plant from which they originally sported.

STOLON. A horizontal stem that produces roots, leaves, or bulbs at the nodes, or a bulb or new plant at the tip.

STRAIN. A group of plants derived from the same parents. The degree of uniformity in a strain depends on the character of the parents, and the number of generations through which selection has been carried on.

TEPAL. A perianth segment. Used to designate both petals and sepals when they look very much alike, as with many bulbous plants.

TETRAPLOID. Having four sets of chromosomes instead of the two sets usually found in plant cells.

TRUMPET. See CORONA.

TUBER. A short swollen part of a stem or shoot, filled with stored food, usually but not always underground, from the surface of which growing shoots can originate.

UMBEL. A flower cluster in which all the stems of the individual flowers radiate from one point.

# Sources of Bulbs

A list of sources offering a wide choice of bulbs, or specialized selections.

Blackthorne Gardens, 48 Quincy St., Holbrook, Mass. Lilies.

The Daffodil Mart, Nuttall, Gloucester, Va. Daffodils, including novelties, small daffodils, and "bushel bargains." Also other spring bulbs.

Allen W. Davis, 3625 S.W. Canby St., Portland 19, Ore. Small bulbs, including crocuses, cyclamens, small daffodils, erythroniums, irises, etc.

P. de Jager & Sons, 188 Asbury St., South Hamilton, Mass. General list, including fine daffodils.

Delkin's Bulbs, 4205 Hunts Point Rd., Bellevue, Washington. Alliums, cyclamens, English iris from seed, erythroniums, etc.

W. J. Dunlop, Broughshane, Ballymena, Northern Ireland. Fine daffodils, including his own originations.

Fairyland Lily Garden, Box 222, Harbor, Ore. Lilies.

J. Heemskerk, care of P. van Deursen, Sassenheim, The Netherlands. General list, daffodils a specialty.

J. M. Jefferson-Brown, Whitbourne, Worcester, England. Choice daffodils.

Walter Marx Gardens, Boring, Ore. General list. Many lilies and the more unusual bulbs.

Grant E. Mitsch, Canby, Ore. Choice daffodils, including his own fine originations.

Charles H. Mueller, River Rd., New Hope, Pa. General list.

H. J. Ohms, Inc., P.O. Box 222, Stamford, Conn. General list.

Beatrice L. Palmer, R.M.D. No. 1, Cobble Hill, Vancouver Island, B.C., Canada. Lilies, including her own and those of Isabella Preston and Dr. Palmer.

## Sources of Bulbs

Pearce Seeds and Plants, Moorestown, N.J. Usual and unusual bulbs.

J. Lionel Richardson, Prospect House, Waterford, Ireland. Choice daffodils, including Mr. Richardson's famous originations.

John Scheepers, Inc., 37 Wall St., New York 5, N.Y. General list.

Skinner's Nursery, Ltd., Dropmore, Manitoba, Canada. Bulbs for cold climates, including Dr. Skinner's own lily originations.

Storecrop Nurseries, Inc., Cold Spring, Putnam County, N.Y. Cyclamens and rock-garden bulbs.

Strawberry Hill Nursery, Rhinebeck, N.Y. Lilies.

Vaughan's Seed Co., 10 W. Randolph St., Chicago 6, Ill., or 24 Vesey St., New York 7, N.Y. General list.

Gerald D. Waltz, P.O. Box 977, Salem, Va. General. Also choice daffodils, including those of Dunlop, Mitsch, Richardson, and Wilson.

Romaine B. Ware, Canby, Ore. Cyclamens, lilies.

Guy L. Wilson, Ltd., Marden, Kent, England. Daffodils of a famous hybridizer.

#### IMPORTATION OF BULBS

Catalogs of foreign firms contain instructions for American customers on the necessary steps needed to order and pay for bulbs. It is easier for the beginning gardener to order from domestic firms, but as gardening interest grows, some like to order special varieties from other countries.

# Good Winter Reading

Bowles, E. A. *Crocus and Colchicum.* New York: D. Van Nostrand Co., 1952.
———. *My Garden in Autumn and Winter.* Dodge, N.Y., 1915.
———. *My Garden in Spring.* Dodge, N.Y., 1914.
———. *My Garden in Summer.* Dodge, N.Y., 1916.
Gray, Alec. *Miniature Daffodils.* Transatlantic Arts, 1961.
Hall, A. D. *The Genus Tulipa.* London: Royal Horticultural Society, 1940.
Jefferson-Brown, J. M. *The Daffodil.* London: Faber & Faber, 1951.
Lawrence, Elizabeth. *The Little Bulbs.* New York: Criterion Books, 1957.
———. *A Southern Garden.* Chapel Hill, N.C.: The University of North Carolina Press, 1942.
Quinn, Carey E. *Daffodils Outdoors and In.* New York: Hearthside Press, 1959.
Rockwell, Grayson, and de Graaff. *The Complete Book of Lilies.* New York: Doubleday & Co., 1961.
Slate, George L. *Lilies for American Gardens.* New York: Charles Scribner's Sons, 1929.
Stern, F. C. *Snowdrops and Snowflakes.* London: Royal Horticultural Society, 1956.
Synge, Patrick M. *Complete Guide to Bulbs.* New York: E. P. Dutton & Co., 1961.
Wilder, Louise Beebe. *Adventures with Hardy Bulbs.* New York: The Macmillan Co., 1936.
Wister, John C. *Bulbs for Home Gardens.* New York: Oxford University Press, 1948.
Woodcock and Stearn. *Lilies of the World.* New York: Charles Scribner's Sons, 1950.

PERIODICALS DEVOTED TO BULBOUS PLANTS

American Daffodil Society Yearbooks
Daffodil and Tulip Yearbooks, Royal Horticultural Society
Lily Yearbooks, Royal Horticultural Society
The North American Lily Society Yearbooks
Bulletins of the National Tulip Society

OCCASIONAL ARTICLES OF UNUSUAL MERIT ON BULBOUS PLANTS

*American Horticultural Magazine*
Bulletins of American Rock Garden Society
Bulletins of Alpine Garden Society (Great Britain)
Bulletins of American Iris Society
*Journal of the Royal Horticultural Society*
*Plants and Gardens* (Brooklyn Botanic Garden Record)

Older garden books are apt to be out of print, but are available to members from the libraries of horticultural societies and garden centers. Some of these libraries will send books to members by mail.

Although culture in Great Britain often differs from culture in the United States for certain plants, British books are an invaluable source of information.

# Index

adder's-tongue, 51
*Allium*, 126-30
*Amarcrinum howardii*, 158
*Amaryllis hallii*, 164
*Anemone*, 48
autumn crocus: *Colchicum*, 159; *Crocus*, 161-62; *Sternbergia*, 165

bluebells, English and Spanish, 124-26; Virginia, 126
bluebottles (grape-hyacinths), 41
*Brodiaea uniflora*, 49-50
bulbs indoors, 166-76; in water, 167-68; in soil, 168-71; care after bloom, 172; precooled and treated bulbs, 172-73; hyacinths, 56-57, 173; daffodils, 174-75; tulips, 175; small bulbs, 175-76
buying bulbs, 16-17

*Camassia*, 130
campernelle, 86-87
checkered-lily, 51
*Chionodoxa*, 40-41
chives, 128
*Colchicum*, 159-61
*Crinodonna corsii*, 158
*Crocus*, 42-46; Dutch, 44; spring species, 45; uses, 45; autumn, 159, 161-62
crown imperial, 50-51
*Cyclamen*, 162-64

daffodils, 58-95; culture, 59-64; transplanting, 63-64; diseases and pests, 64-68; choosing, 68; jonquil, 69, 83, 86, 94; classification, 70-71; varieties, 71-87; trumpets, 70, 71-73, 93; poet's narcissus, 85-87; "Paper White," 85, 167; campernelle, 86; pheasant's eye, 87; uses, 87-91; small daffodils, 92-95; hoop-petticoat, 95; planting depths, 95; companion plants, 95
depth of planting, *see* planting depths
diseases, 32; daffodil, 64-68; tulip, 101-02; lily, 140-44
dogtooth-violet, 51-52
drainage, 26-27

*Endymion*, 125-26
*Eranthis*, 46-47
*Erythronium*, 51-52

fertilizers, 28-29
first bulb order, 17-20
foliage, care of, 33-34
forcing, 166-76; *see* bulbs indoors
*Fritillaria*, 50

*Galanthus*, 38
glacier-lily, 52
glory-of-the-snow, 40-41
goldband lily, 135, 152
grape-hyacinths, 41-42
guinea-hen flower, 51

hardy amaryllis, 164

## Index

humus, *see* organic matter
hyacinth, 53-57; uses, 53; species, 54-55; Dutch, 55-57; culture (Dutch), 55-56; varities (Dutch), 56-57; forcing, 56-57, 173-74

*Ipheion uniflorum,* 50
importations, 184
iris, early, 48-49; Dutch, 122-23; Spanish, 123-24; English, 124

jonquil, 69; garden varieties, 83; wild species, 86-87

Lebanon squill, 42
*Leucojum,* 39
lily, 132-57; buying and planting, 136-38; care, 138-40; pests and diseases, 140-45; beginner's choices, 146-48; other hybrids, 148-51; species, 151-54; uses, 155-57
*Lycoris,* 164-65

madonna lily, 135, 152
*Mertensia virginica,* 126
*Muscari,* 41-42

*Narcissus* (daffodil), 58-95; poet's, 85-87; "Paper White," 85, 167-68; *see also* daffodil
*Nerine sarniensis,* 164

onion, 126-30
organic matter, 25
*Ornithogalum,* 130-31

"Paper White," 85, 167
pests, 32–33; crocus, 46; daffodil, 66-68; tulip, 101-02; lily, 144-45
pheasant's eye narcissus, 87
planting, 30-31; depths, 31; small bulbs, 36-37

*Puschkinia scilloides,* 42

regal lily, 135, 153
rodents, 32-33

*Scilla:* early, 39-40; late, 124-25
snake's-head, 51
snowdrops, 38-39
snowflakes, 39
soils, 23-27
sources of bulbs, 183-84
special plant societies, 21
spider-lily, 164
spring star-flower, 49-50
squills, 39-40
star-of-Bethlehem: *Ipheion,* 50; *Ornithogalum,* 130-31
*Sternbergia lutea,* 165
striped squill, 42
subsoil, 26
sun, 29-30

*Tritelia uniflora,* 49-50
trout-lily, 51-52
tulips, 96-120; culture, 98-101; diseases and pests, 101-02, 110-11; classification and varieties, 102-16; early, 103-04; double, 104, 113-14; Mendel, 105; triumph, 105-06; Darwin, breeder, and cottage, 106-09; lily-flowered, 109-10; parrot, 112-13; broken (Rembrandt, bizarre, bijbloemen), 110-11; oddities, 111-12; species and species hybrids, 114-17; uses, 117-20; forcing, 175

water, 27
windflower, 48
winter-aconite, 46-47
wood-hyacinth, 124-25